AF849262

# Blockchain for Halal Industry

Hussein Elasrag

Blockchain for Halal Industry

Hussein Elasrag

Copyright©2019 Hussein Elasrag

First edition in 2019

Second edition in 2022

The global halal market has emerged as a new growth sector in the global economy and is creating a strong presence in developed countries. The halal industry has now expanded well beyond the food sector further widening the economic potentials for halal. This book aims to provide an introduction to applying Blockchain for halal supply chains and outline some potential areas for consideration for the all sectors of the halal industry. The book will help to deepen understanding of the concepts of Blockchain technology and halal industry and explores the concept of Halal industry along with the components which constitute the industry. The book Provides and discusses existing halal supply chains usage of Blockchains... The opportunities and challenges in developing and Halal industry are also discussed...

# Contents

# I. Introduction

The blockchain technology is rapidly gaining the attention of Organizations of Islamic Cooperation. There are various Islamic financial institutes which are planning to use the blockchain system to bring the benefits that come with it.

In PwC's 2018 survey of 600 executives from 15 territories, 84% say their organizations have at least some involvement with blockchain technology. Companies have dabbled in the lab; perhaps they've built proofs of concept. Everyone is talking about blockchain, and no one wants to be left behind. It's easy to see why. As a distributed, tamperproof ledger, a well-designed blockchain doesn't just cut out intermediaries, reduce costs, and increase speed and reach. It also offers greater transparency and traceability for many business processes. Gartner forecasts that blockchain will generate an annual business value of more than US $3 trillion by 2030. It's possible to imagine that 10% to 20% of global economic infrastructure will be running on blockchain-based systems by that same year.

For the Islamic economy, blockchain technology has the potential to make a significant impact. The blockchain in Islamic finance and banking will surely help the Islamic banks, and financial institutes to succeed. Without worry about the interest and other such issues Islamic banking system will be able to work more productively.

Islamic financial institutions are increasingly using blockchain technology for complex financing terms, Shariah-compliant transactions and Islamic and sharia-compliant alternatives to conventional insurance. back-office automation, and underwriting of micro-insurance. Islamic finance can use cryptocurrencies for SMEs finance, underpinned by blockchain technology, to structure payments in an efficient and cost-effective manner.

The installation of blockchain in halal supply chains will primarily affect the way payments, remittances and trading activities are conducted. This technology is moving forward towards the mainstream and promises to provide benefits in several areas. It can:

- Modernize legal documentation through the application of smart contracts
- Significantly reduce transaction processing time

- Reduce costs for providers, and transaction fees for consumers
- Eliminate the need for documentation and manual reconciliation of transactions
- Reduce the need for centralized regulation
- Eliminate the risk of errors and duplication
- Reduce or eradicate fraud
- Manage counterparty risk

Blockchain's core attributes mean that it has significant potential for use in Islamic finance due to its:

- Transparency: blockchain provides provenance, traceability and transparency of transactions
- Control: access to permissioned networks is restricted to identified users
- Security: the digital ledger cannot be altered or tampered with once the data is entered. Fraud is less likely and easier to spot
- Real-time information: when information is updated, it's updated for everyone in the network at the same time

It must first be stated that the Islamic dietary and consumption system is different and unique compared to other ethnic dietary systems. The world community has now begun to understand the importance of the

Muslims requirement for food and other consumption known as halal. The market for certified halal food and products is growing robustly, both domestically and internationally. Although the term halal has never attracted as much attention as in recent times, today, wherever there are Muslim consumers whose tastes and preferences are governed by halal rules on food specification, a halal food market exists. Every Muslim must ensure that what they eat comes from a halal source. This does not mean only to check the ingredients per se, but also to ensure that the whole process is in accordance with Shariah principles.(Zakaria 2008)

Halal is an Arabic word meaning lawful and permitted. This Halal concept comes from the Holy Quran which it uses to describe objects and actions. Islam is a natural way of life and encompasses the concept of an economic system based on human cooperation and brotherhood, which is based on the consultation and dietary laws for all humanity. Halal consists of anything that is free from any component that Muslims are prohibited from consuming. This can be classified as 'pork free' in its physical existence, including food substances such as gelatin, enzymes, lecithin and glycerin as well additives such as flavorings and coloring.(Zakaria 2008, Hj Hassan 2013)

Halal is a Quranic term that means permitted, allowed, lawful or legal. Its opposite is haram (forbidden, unlawful or illegal). According to Shari'ah, all issues concerning Halal or Haram and even all disputes should be referred to Quran and Sunnah. Halal and Haram are universal terms that apply to all aspects of human life whether is related to his ibadat or muamalat or mua'sharah. Halal may be defined as an act, object or conduct over which the individual has freedom of choice and its exercise does not carry either a reward or a punishment. Halal may have been identified by explicit evidence in the Shari'ah or by reference to the presumption of permissibility (ibahah). At the global level, the Food and Agriculture Organization of the United Nations has prepared general guidelines for use of the term halal to be adopted by member countries. (Ager, Abdullah et al.)

Basic principles for Halal products are:(Malboobi and Malboobi 2012)

1. Being Halal or Haram products is the function of being lawful or unlawful with respect to Divine orders.

2. Assigning Halal or Haram depends on being

beneficial or harmful, respectively.

3. In the context of the above concepts, assigned orders in Shari'ah are both fixed and variable rules based on the state of subjects on specific times and places.

4. Orders in Shari'ah are ranked based on the degree of being beneficial or harmful while the best choice is preferred whenever it is necessary.

5. Some controls and governing regulations such as "La dirar" (no harm to human), Haraj (the existence of serious threat and/or constraints), and urgency rules occasionally disapprove the orders.

Therefore, especially Muslims are responsible to embrace of this order more than anyone. This is a faith issue for them. Due to it is a faith issue of Muslims, non-Muslims can never deal with Halal and Tayyib standardization and certification. No one can abuse this for their commercial and ideology. Non-Muslims can never be involved in Halal and Tayyib certification as they can't be an imam at the mosque in prayers.

It is thus important for the world community, both Muslim and non- Muslim, to recognize the potential of the Halal industry. This is because delving into an emerging billion-dollar industry such as the Halal industry could help to further develop the economy just as it would serve to solve some of the long-standing problems faced by the Muslim community. There are reasons why the Halal industry is important to world's growth as a multi-racial society. Many Muslims and non-Muslims consumers still do not understand the spirit of Shari'ah governing these products. Halal principles are not confined to the strictly religious, but involve health, cleanliness and safety.

This book aims to provide an introduction to applying Blockchain for halal supply chains and outline some potential areas for consideration for the all sectors of the halal industry. The book will help to deepen understanding of the concepts of Blockchain technology and halal industry and explores the concept of Halal industry along with the components which constitute the industry. The book Provides and discusses existing halal supply chains usage of Blockchains... The opportunities and challenges in developing and Halal industry are also discussed...

## II. The Halal Economy and The Market Opportunity

The global halal industry is estimated to be worth around USD2.3 trillion (excluding Islamic finance). Growing at an estimated annual rate of 20%, the industry is valued at about USD560 billion a year. Thus, making it one of the fastest growing consumer segments in the world. The global halal market of 1.8 billion Muslims is no longer confined to food and food related products. The halal industry has now expanded beyond the food sector to include pharmaceuticals, cosmetics, health products, toiletries and medical devices as well as service sector components such as logistics, marketing, print and electronic media, packaging, branding, and financing.(Fleishman Hillard Majlis 2011, Dar, Azmi et al. 2013)

In recent years, with the increase in the number of affluent Muslims, the halal industry has expanded further into lifestyle offerings including halal travel and hospitality services as well as fashion. This development has been triggered by the change in the mind set of Muslim consumers as well as ethical consumer trends worldwide.

The halal market is non-exclusive to Muslims, and has gained increasing acceptance among non-Muslim consumers who associate halal with ethical consumerism. As such, the values promoted by halal - social responsibility, stewardship of the earth, economic and social justice, animal welfare and ethical investment - have gathered interest beyond its religious compliance. The popularity of, and demand for, halal certified products among non-Muslim consumers have been on the rise as more consumers are looking for high quality, safe and ethical products.

No longer a mere religious obligation or observance for Muslims, halal (which means "lawful" or "allowable") has become a powerful market force, becoming increasingly a world-wide market phenomenon for both Muslims and non-Muslims alike. The appendage of "Halal" to a product is not just a guarantee that the product is permitted for Muslims, but it has also become a global symbol for quality assurance and lifestyle choice. This is evident by the participation and involvement of non- Muslim countries and organizations where halal is fast emerging as the standard of choice. Many Western countries have recognized the emerging global trend in consumerism towards halal products and services, and are now racing to gain a footing in the halal industry.(Dar, Azmi et al. 2013)

Based on a report from the United Nations, Islam is the 2nd largest religion after Christianity. UN statistics recorded yearly growth of Muslims at around 6.4% compared to 1.46% for Christianity. According to the same statistics, 1 in 5 persons in this world is a Muslim by birth or geography. Based on the statistics earlier, Muslims presents a huge global market for halal products and services and since Muslims in general adhere strongly to religious principles and are increasingly particular and sensitive over the halalness of their life style, especially food, the prospect for halal market is enormous. Therefore, to tap into the vast opportunity which the halal industry presents, several aspects concerning the halal concept must be taken into account by all, including non-Muslim businessmen. The following measures present a winning approach for the halal business industry to gain competitive advantage in this promising and lucrative market.(Awang, Abdul-Rahim et al. 2014)

Muslims represent an estimated 23% of the global population or about

1.8 billion consumers with an average growth rate of 3% per annum.(Dar, Azmi et al. 2013)

This market provides huge potential for companies, organizations and others, from the west and from Muslim countries, and is on a steep growth path. The global Muslim population is expected to grow by about 35 percent over the next 20 years, rising from 1.6 billion in 2010 to 2.2 billion by 2030, or 26.4 percent of the world's total projected population of 8.3 billion. By 2050, the Muslim population could grow to

2.6 billion and represent nearly 30 percent of the global projected population.(Fleishman Hillard Majlis 2011)

Also by 2030, 79 countries are expected to hold a million or more Muslim residents, as opposed to the current 72 countries. Although many western business executives may not realize it, a majority of the world's Muslims (more than 60 percent) will continue to live in the Asia Pacific region, while about 20 percent will live in the Middle East and North Africa. Muslims will remain relatively small minorities in Europe and the Americas, but will constitute a growing share of the total population in these regions. To be successful in Asia, as well as the Middle East and North Africa, western companies must learn to understand and address the Muslim market on a large scale.(Fleishman Hillard Majlis 2011)

One demographic factor makes the Muslim market particularly attractive to a variety of companies – it is largely young and part of an emerging middle class on the road to greater consumption. Islamic doctrine, by and large, is not ascetic and does not discourage trade or consumerism. Likewise, it does not divide the state from religion, which means that Muslims practice their faith hand in hand with the political, social and cultural roles they play in society.

In Islamic majority and minority countries throughout Asia, the Middle East, Africa, and Europe, business activity is escalating, with Islamic trade currently estimated in trillions of dollars.

Companies are coming to understand the great opportunity that the Muslim consumer represents. But addressing this market is not as straightforward as dealing with other billion population consumer markets such as India and China. For a start, the Muslim community is not a single homogeneous group. Muslims live in every country in the world, represent every race and come from every social and economic stratum. And although they share the common thread of their beliefs, they have their own cultural, regional or local nuances, preferences and practices.

Although Islam is often associated with the Arab world and the Middle East, this region is home to only 20% of the world's Muslim population. This number is expected to grow by more than a third in the next two decades.

Sub-Saharan Africa make up 15% of Muslims worldwide and is projected to grow by nearly 60% in the next two decades. About one-fifth of Muslims live in a country or region where they are the minority. Although Muslims will remain a minority group in Europe and Americas, they will constitute a growing share of the total population.5 Europe's Muslim community is expected to increase by nearly a third from 44.1 million in 2010 to 58.2 million in 2030. In the Americas, the number of Muslims is expected to double during the same period.

The sizeable and growing Muslim consumer market across the globe will continue to fuel the halal industry's double digit growth, creating a plethora of opportunities in the market for halal products and services.

Increasing awareness of Muslim consumers on their religious obligations has also contributed to the increasing demand for halal products and services. The demographics of Muslims have undergone significant change in recent years. There is now a wave of religious fervor amongst the rising social class of young, highly educated, savvy and affluent Muslims, who embraces an "Islamic contemporary with global lifestyle." This new generation of Muslims favors Western-style products and aspires to a modern lifestyle as they become more integrated into the global economy as consumers, employees, travelers, investors, manufacturers, retailers and traders. This has created a worldwide demand for mainstream products and services that conform to Islamic values.

The diversity of the Muslim consumer can prove to be a challenge to those who view markets as geographies and for whom the concept of an Islamic consciousness operating across market frontiers is alien. Neither can the Muslim economy be as easily defined as other cross- border markets such as the "green economy" or the "pink dollar".

Economist Ben Simpfendorfer suggests that the strong cultural and historical links between the Muslim and non-Muslim worlds are starting to come to the fore. He gives the example of China as a country that is addressing the Muslim opportunity.(Fleishman Hillard Majlis 2011)

In his book, "The New Silk Road", he cites the example of the city of Yiwu where an estimated 200,000 Arab nationals visit the Chinese coastal city every year because it boasts the largest wholesale consumer goods market in China. What sets Yiwu apart is that it has made commerce convenient, particularly for Muslim buyers from the Middle East and beyond. Besides products that appeal to Muslim consumers, Yiwu's success lies in an open arms approach that the Chinese government has shown to Muslim traders and consumers. A prayer hall for nearly 10,000 worshippers has been constructed by the government, Halal food is easily available, while clerics appointed and subsidized by the government lead prayers - this at a time when governments in the west are questioning minarets on Mosques (Switzerland) or public prayer gatherings (France).(Fleishman Hillard Majlis 2011)

For brands that find ways to embrace and engage the

Muslim consumer, the rewards are rich. And smart, compelling communications will play a critical role in targeting a consumer market that already represents nearly a quarter of humanity.

Much has already been written about Islamic finance and the Halal opportunity, and in more depth than we cover. Our purpose in this report is to flag up the development of the opportunity, highlight where the greatest potential lies and analyze the communications and reputation issues that companies need to be aware of.

While the market has many facets and niche segments, understanding the umbrella term "Halal" is fundamental to approaching this market.

The largest opportunity within the Halal market is undoubtedly food, which is also where the greatest challenge lies. Indeed, the term Halal has become synonymous, in some Muslim minority countries, with food and is almost universally associated with the ritual slaughter (or Zabiah) of animals. This has narrowed the discourse around Halal, limiting the focus of many organizations and contributing to misunderstandings and reputational issues.(Fleishman Hillard Majlis 2011)

In the view of some non-Muslims, Halal goes against general sensibilities by requiring all blood to be extracted from meat (in much the same way as Kosher food). Thus, Halal, to some audiences, has become a negative word. But, given the size of the market and the relative ease with which food can be 'converted' to Halal, some companies have quietly introduced 'Halal by stealth'. But this has only exacerbated the problem and, in the view of this report, held back the wider availability and acceptance of Halal products.

Modern day living is largely influenced by science and technology and subsequently this has impacted the halal aspect of daily activities. It is human nature to desire everything that is good in life in the form of clothing, food, housing, interaction with fellow human beings and healthy environment. In Islam, anything which is halal brings goodness and prosperity for mankind is not detrimental to life and in effect, it elevates man to a higher level in this world.

On the other hand, something which is haram is perceived as physically and spiritually impure, inferior and defective, traits which are naturally repulsive to mankind. Anything haram constitutes harmful elements which affect man's psychology and his physical well-being. Research which integrates the halal concept with science focuses on universal benefits, the natural disposition of man, health, cleanliness and quality. The halal concept encapsulates the universal nature of Islam. Thus, scientific research relating to the halal concept is commendable.(Awang, Abdul-Rahim et al. 2014)

Respect the beliefs of others: Non-Muslim food manufactures must be aware of and respect Muslims beliefs and principles regarding halal which include food, clothing, financial transaction and others. It is part of a belief system and moral code of conduct integral to the daily living of Muslims. Therefore, it would be unwise and detrimental for the manufactures to purposely challenge the Muslims by introducing non-halal elements into the food, clothing and services claimed to be halal, since this will erode the confidence of the consumers and consequently decrease the integrity of these products and pose a challenge to the growth of this market.(Awang, Abdul-Rahim et al. 2014)

## III. Segments of the Halal Market

It must first be stated that the Islamic dietary and consumption system is different and unique compared to other ethnic dietary systems. The world community has now begun to understand the importance of the Muslims requirement for food and other consumption known as halal. The market for certified halal food and products is growing robustly, both domestically and internationally. Although the term halal has never attracted as much attention as in recent times, today, wherever there are Muslim consumers whose tastes and preferences are governed by halal rules on food specification, a halal food market exists. Every Muslim must ensure that what they eat comes from a halal source. This does not mean only to check the ingredients per se, but also to ensure that the whole process is in accordance with Shari'ah principles.(Zakaria 2008)

### 1. Food

Driven by growing demand, the Halal food market continues to build its momentum across the global food supply chain. The State of the Global Islamic Economy Report 2015/16 estimates that Market size and profile

— Global Muslim consumer spending on food & beverage at $1,128 billion (17% of global expenditure):

The Report estimates global Muslim spending on food and beverages (F&B) to be $1,128 billion in 2014. The total global F&B spending during the same period is estimated to be $6,755 billion in 2014, making the Muslim food market 16.7% of global expenditure.

Comparatively, this is a 4.3% increase from 2013 Muslim F&B expenditure that was $1,081 billion (reflecting the adjusted projections methodology). The Muslim Food expenditure is expected to grow to

$1,585 billion market by 2020 and will account for 16.9% of global expenditure. This equates to a 2014-20 CAGR growth of 5.8%.

Based on total food consumption, the top countries with Muslim food consumption are Indonesia ($158 billion), Turkey ($110 billion), Pakistan ($100.5 billion), and Iran ($59 billion) based on 2014 estimates. Comparatively, the collective global Muslim F&B market is larger than the F&B consumption of the top geographical markets in 2014, such as China ($797.8 billion), United States ($741.2 billion), Japan ($367.3 billion) and India ($335.7 billion). Geographically 16% of Muslim food consumption is in non-OIC member countries. A testament to this sector's strength is that the success of the Halal food market remains constant across different cultures and continents. In Malaysia, Nestle Malaysia and its Halal Centre of Excellence have become the biggest producers of Halal products in the world. In the United States of America, Saffron Road with its Halal and organic produce has become the model of success for both Muslim and non Muslim aspiring entrepreneurs. From Asia to America, the Halal food sector is becoming a major source of growth in both the Islamic and wider global economy. Of course, there are challenges as well. There is a continuing struggle for Halal food standards and accreditation, with more education required of such topics in OIC countries. The recent ban on Halal and Kosher slaughter in Denmark along with scare stories about Halal food in the media reflect a current attitude prevalent in Europe and increasingly in the United States that is suspicious of Muslim and Islamic customs and rituals in the public square. Engaging and overcoming these challenges will be pivotal to the future success of the Halal food sector.(Thomson Reuters and Dinar Standard 2016)

The halal marketplace is emerging as one of the most profitable and influential market arenas in the world food business today. The halal food market has grown strongly over the past decade and is now worth an estimated USD667 million. Halal food represents close to 20% of the entire global food industry. With expected increases in both population and income of halal consumers, and coupled with the expected increase in demand for food by more than 70% by 2050, the future demand for halal food is strong.

Many food economists posit that the halal food industry will become a major market force in the near future based on four prevalent trends. Firstly, Islam is now the fastest growing religion in the world thus fueling a global demand for halal products. The annual growth in consumption of halal food is estimated at 16%. Secondly, the increasing trend of consuming halal food products for ethical and safety reasons by non-Muslim consumers. In the UK, for example, there are over 2 million Muslims, yet there are 6 million consumers of halal meat.8 In the Netherlands, non-Muslim Dutch consumers have shown marked interest in halal food where total demand is estimated to reach about USD3 billion on an annual basis.9 These two factors combined have made halal products mainstream consumer goods. Third is the rising halal consumer power as a market force in tandem with the growth of the Muslim population and their rising disposable income. Finally, there is greater awareness among Muslims on the need and necessity to consume only halal food. A good example of such increasing consumer awareness is the rapid rise in annual sales of halal food throughout Russia and the growing demand for halal products between 30% and 40% annually.

Until a decade ago, halal food products were offered in traditional corner shops and neighborhood butchers. The halal market has witnessed a universal shift in the demand and supply chains of halal food products. They are increasingly made available in Western-style grocery stores including supermarkets and hypermarket chains. In many western countries, supermarkets and food producers are starting to reach out to Muslim consumers by offering a wider selection of halal food products. Halal food is becoming an increasing part of the Western diet and has become a multi-billion dollar global industry involving multinationals like Tesco, Unilever and Nestlé who have aggressively expanded their halal-certified product lines. To date, Nestle is the biggest food manufacturer in the halal sector with annual sales of more than USD5 billion. Halal food accounts for about 35% of Nestle's global sales.

From a market perspective, the traditional major target markets remain in Asia and the Middle East. However, halal markets in the UK, Europe and the USA will see their roles in the development of the halal market significantly enhanced as they are markets that play defining roles in other markets around the world. It will bring halal into the global mainstream. As the dynamics within the Muslim world change and globalization trends continue to shape consumers' tastes, habit and spending patterns across the world; it is highly likely that the developing halal markets will have increasingly influential roles in the established markets of the Middle East and Asia particularly by influencing global corporate halal strategies.

It is not surprising that the biggest halal food manufacturers and exporters are located in non-Muslims countries like the US, Brazil, Argentina, Australia and China. Because of the traditional nature of the market, it is estimated that multinationals from these countries control 90% of the global halal market. In Malaysia, for example, Muslim consumers spent an average 14% of their food budget on meat. 60% of the halal meat is imported from India, Australia and New Zealand. Other Muslim countries including Saudi Arabia, Algeria and Egypt also import meat from non-Muslim countries to meet their local consumption demand. Countries like Brazil, Argentina, New Zealand and Australia have established themselves as market leaders in the export of halal meat and poultry.

Halal food products are not confined to meat and poultry, including other food items such as confectionary, canned and frozen food, dairy produce, bakery products, organic food, beverages and herbal products. The evolving lifestyle and increase in purchasing powers of Muslims means that there is widespread demand for prepared convenience foods as well as packaged foodstuff that still conform to Islamic dietary laws. Another growing sector of foods is comprised of substitutes for products that traditionally contain non-halal (haram) ingredients such as pork gelatin or alcohol. These products, which include yogurt, biscuits, and chocolates, are now being modified so that they can be marketed as halal.

Global Halal Food : Key Challenges and Opportunities

Challenges

↘↘ There is ongoing confusion surrounding Halal standards, primarily because they are being produced by so many different government- linked organizations; private organizations and independent Halal certification bodies (HCB's); national standards bodies, regional bodies such as ASEAN, GSO and the EU; and international bodies such as the SMIIC/OIC initiative. The challenge for manufacturers is to determine which standard will actually provide market access, and in too many cases multiple certificates are necessary for exporters.

↘↘ The absence of any viable international schemes to accredit Halal certification bodies (HCBs) has long been a problem for the Halal industry. The majority of Halal food is being produced in Non-Muslim majority countries, and is certified by independent HCB's that operate with little regulatory oversight. Current accreditation initiatives, such as being developed by SMIIC, GSO and ESMA are all moves in the right direction, more coordination between the accreditation bodies is needed to avoid unnecessary duplication or competition.

↘↘ Difficulty in obtaining Shari'ah-compliant funding. Companies wishing to scale or to vertically integrate their supply chain face challenges in obtaining Shari'ah-compliant funding.

Opportunities (Thomson Reuters and Dinar Standard 2016)

↘ OIC countries that have expertise in Halal food processes have an opportunity to develop partnerships with non-OIC countries eager to strengthen their Halal capabilities. Countries such as China, South Korea and South Africa are already partnering with Malaysia and the UAE to develop their Halal capabilities.

↘↘ An opportunity to develop tracking technology. Verifying supply- chain integrity is a major challenge that comes up when we speak to experts in this space. One way to overcome this is by developing tracking technology that raw meat and food ingredients to their source. The Brazilian Meat Exporting Industries Association (ABIEC) developed a device called the e-seal that tracks meat cargo passing through their ports.

↘↘ An increased demand for hormone free meat. Regulators differ on whether hormone treated meat is permissible. There is debate among experts on how safe such meat is for human consumption, with concerns of cancer, and other side effects. Following interest from customers on hormones, the UAE supermarket chain Spinneys, is the first to sell hormone free meat.

↘↘ Halal food has the opportunity to be the global standard for safe, wholesome, humane food if producers fully adhered to the concept of Halal and Tayyib as in the tenets of Islam. There is an increased global demand for organic and natural food which is starting to appear among Muslim consumers, especially the younger millennial generation. While it may involve the higher cost of producing farm-raised, organic-fed meat, versus of the cheaper options many Muslims may look for; despite these challenges, this is a long term goal Muslim producers should strive to achieve. Included in this is the potential of developing premier quality innovative Halal brands for this new generation of Muslim consumers. Just as organic was a fringe market 10 years ago, but is now found in mainstream supermarkets, and just like made-in- Japan in the 50's was synonymous with low quality, but with the combined efforts of Japanese manufacturer, backed by national support, it now stands for the highest quality.

↘↘ Develop premium organic product lines. There is an increased global demand for organic and natural food. This heightened interest is also starting to appear among Muslim consumers, especially the younger millennial generation.

↘↘ Develop strong brands. There is much room for improvement in the branding of even popular brands. Product quality, marketing messaging, packaging and overall communication can be greatly enhanced. This provides an opportunity for either existing brands to step up their game as well as for new players to differentiate through powerful branding.

↘↘ Investment opportunities in Halal food value chain integration. Many companies in the Halal food market are small and fragmented. Financing vertical integration of the supply chain, from slaughterhouses to distributors is an investment opportunity that should provide lucrative returns for the investors as well as develop strong companies in this space.

## 2. Pharmaceutical and health products

Pharmaceutical and health products are also large growth areas in the global halal industry. Demand for halal pharmaceutical, generic medial, wellness and healthcare products are estimated to be about USD555 billion in Muslim-majority countries. The main concern among Muslims is the use of non-compliant substances such as animal derivatives and animal-based gelatins in these products. The global market growth for pharmaceuticals increased by 4% in 2009 to a value that exceeded USD820 billion, offering vast potential opportunities for the halal pharmaceutical industry to tap into. The rising healthcare costs also provide the halal market with a key differentiation factor in the supply of generic pharmaceuticals.

pharmaceutical ingredients and product integrity analytical methodology. In the move to strengthen the integrity within the manufacturing and servicing of medicines and health supplements, Malaysia introduced a new standard for halal pharmaceuticals. "The Malaysian Standard MS2424:2010 (P): Halal

Pharmaceuticals General Guidelines" addresses the entire pharmaceutical industry's supply chain from processing to handling, packaging, labelling, distribution, storage and display of medicines and health supplements.

### 3. Cosmetics

Growth in the halal cosmetics market is mirrored by a growth in consumer knowledge about the ingredients used and product awareness, fueled by social networks.13 The global halal cosmetic industry is estimated at USD13 billion with an annual growth rate of 12%.14 At present the halal cosmetic market constitutes 11% of the total global halal industry. The emerging halal cosmetic and personal care market is seen by analysts as next in line for growth after the lucrative halal food sector. The main driver for this huge demand in halal cosmetics and beauty products stems from the demographic of young, religiously conscious, and dynamic professional Muslim population. In the scope of halal cosmetics, the concept covers critical aspects of production such as halal ingredients and usage of permissible substances which must be manufactured, stored, packaged and delivered in conformity with Shari requirements. Interestingly, halal cosmetics has also gained momentum amongst modern consumers who are eco-ethical conscious and are willing to pay a premium for organic, natural and earthy cosmetics products to suit their modern lifestyle.

The market for halal cosmetics is booming in the Middle East and Asia. Across the Middle East, halal cosmetics are registering a 12% annual growth reaching USD12 billion in total value of cosmetic related sales. Markets in Asia, particularly Malaysia and Indonesia as well as Europe, have seen a surge in interest in halal cosmetics. In Malaysia, halal cosmetics contribute 10% – 20% of the local cosmetics market. However, the global cosmetics industry is dominated, and to a certain degree monopolized, by non-Muslims companies. This poses serious challenges to the issue of halal ingredients in cosmetic products manufactured by the companies.

Although Muslims are generally allowed to consume haram (forbidden) products in life threatening situations, the demand for pharmaceuticals that adhere to Muslim rules is growing. The increasing global demand in halal pharmaceuticals is in tandem with the growing interest and concerns of Muslims concerning the halal status of pharmaceuticals. Many of them are challenging the industry on the origins of the ingredients of these products and whether they are compliant with an Islamic lifestyle. Halal pharmaceutical products should not only be free from haram constituents, but they should also be tayyib which is a term given to goods and products which meet quality standards. In general, tayyib refers to products that are clean, pure and produced based on standard processes and procedures. Thus, a pharmaceutical product should not only be halal, but should also be judged clean according to Shari'a law.

However, the halal pharmaceutical market is plagued with the lack of global halal standards on Many cosmetic products contain alcohol which is deemed as haram, and animal sourced components considered impure by Islam. Growing concerns about animal-derived ingredients such as gelatin and collagen in cosmetic products are fueling demand from both Muslim and non-Muslims consumers. The halal label on cosmetics and beauty products appeal to consumers seeking integrity and authenticity in their cosmetic and personal care products. Although the concept of halal cosmetics is very new to the Muslim world, there is a growing demand especially from conscientious consumers who are becoming more selective in their choice of personal care items, and consciously choosing to spend money on cosmetics and beauty products that fit in with their religious and cultural requirements.

Halal cosmetics have developed far beyond a novelty. Capitalizing on the burgeoning halal cosmetic market, a number of cosmetic companies are beginning to develop this niche market by producing halal- certified product lines that contain no animal ingredients, and not tested on animals to meet the growing demand of consumers who simply want more assurance that the cosmetics they are using are healthy and sustainably sourced. A challenge to further develop this niche halal sector is on how to best integrate halal cosmetics into the framework of the global beauty industry. Active collaboration with key parallel interest groups such as organic, vegan, ethical and environmental rights may be key to further strengthen the value of halal cosmetic products in the global market.

**Pharmaceuticals and Cosmetics Sector : Key Challenges and Opportunities**

Challenges: (Thomson Reuters and Dinar Standard 2016)

↘↘ Rapid developments in synthetic biology in the future are causing concern — i.e. from microorganisms and plants of the future that have been genetically engineered to the extreme to contain large parts, and potentially complete, edited/synthetic genomes (in other words man- made designer microorganisms and plants). This will not only impact antibiotics but also future food produced from such 'synthetic' organisms. Though this is for the future, authorities are already looking into how to regulate such developments.

↘↘ Many Muslim auditors are not trained in Good Manufacturing Practices (GMP) guidelines, which are important for maintaining quality. The use of Good Manufacturing Practices (GMP) guidelines that correspond with a country's legislation for cosmetics and personal care products have been designed to improve product quality and tractability to protect human life and help ensure that products are pure and healthy (tayyib). It is not just a case of detecting haram ingredients but also the unethical masbooh ingredients (best to avoid) because of damaging effects from them absorbed through the skin or internally with medication. Many Muslim auditors may not be trained in GMP guidelines so may miss potential points of contamination. Ensuring that Halal auditors and technical experts have this training is essential for the growth of Halal certified personal care and pharmaceuticals.

↘↘ Alcohol which is used in various forms, both for the maintenance of machinery and in the products themselves, is one aspect in Halal standard guidelines that differs between countries. Whether the views can be standardized on this remains to be seen.

↘↘ The use of ingredients in cosmetics that are toxic to the human being may be considered to be Haram in Halal certification as they are not tayyib. For example, some of the ingredients used in skin whitening creams, such as hydroquinone and mercury come under this category. These ingredients are banned in many countries but are still in use in some countries. They are considered toxic inside the body so are also harmful on the outside of the body. They kill the melanin cells that, among other things, can cause cancer.

↘↘ Challenge to get funding for research and development. Horizon 2020 is the biggest EU Research and Innovation program ever with nearly €80 billion of funding available over 7 years (2014 to 2020). The main problem with Horizon 2020 (and other government and European funding schemes) is not that they are very competitive but that they are very thematic — i.e. the call subjects are not 'open'. The topics are decided upon and prioritized by the authorities a good couple of years in advance. When the topics of the calls come out the type of research we intend to do in Halal is not called for and hence we cannot fit our Halal ideas directly to a topic 'on the table'. We need to influence the future calls by invoking some ways to getting the topics important to the Muslim and other faith communities.

Opportunities (Thomson Reuters and Dinar Standard 2016)

↘↘ There are many opportunities to educate both consumers and producers in Muslim countries about the transdermal (skin penetrating) nature of some types of cosmetics. In western countries, there are safety guidelines that require any new types of ingredients in cosmetics, such as nanoparticles, be fully tested to show that they are safe in humans. In Muslim countries, these safety considerations are secondary to Halal considerations. We tend to look at ingredients from porcine sources as being considered Haram, or Najis (ritually unclean) as they can be washed off the skin. However, safety in humans should also be a consideration in Halal guidelines for cosmetics. New technologies, like nanoparticles being used in creams, face powders, etc., are currently being debated by the European Medicines Agency (EMA) from a safety perspective, but in Muslim countries we are lagging far behind the West. Currently, research on new technologies, materials and their safety in humans is exclusively done by the non-Muslim countries and funded by non-Muslims. This is an excellent opportunity for Muslim scientists and investors to lead and gain expertise in research in these fields to promote and determine the Halal status of these technologies.

↘↘ Opportunity to market Halal cosmetics to non-Muslim consumers. Most Halal cosmetics focus on natural ingredients, eco-friendliness and fair trade. Some are also vegan, so there is an opportunity to market them to non-Muslims. Both UK-based PHB Ethical Beauty and Ecotrail, the Indian company behind the Iba brand, target a wider consumer base with products that are not only Halal certified but also cruelty-free, and free from harsh chemicals and in the case of Iba are organic and free of animal-derived products.

↘↘ Opportunity to resolve the issue of the scarcity of Halal gelatin by working out a practical solution to utilize the relevant parts from sacrificed animals during Hajj. Halal options could also be available from using vegetable derived substitutes. For example, the pharma industry has become fixated with using gelatin for capsule production because it is low cost, cheap and has been used for many years. The market needs educating for more natural alternatives such as alginates, pectins, etc which can be reformulated to offer the same physical properties.

↘↘ There is a need to develop and publish a Halal Pharmacopoeia and other references for industry players to supplement Halal pharmaceutical standards.

↘↘ The five keys to becoming a successful pharmaceutical company are: Having the best sourcing and manufacturing capabilities; the second is to find the best regulatory team to understand and navigate regulations; the third is deep customer insights; the fourth is for customer insights to lead the core product line; and the fifth is to have a consistent Research and Development (R&D) investment to create new and innovative products.

↘↘ Inter-Islamic country fast track registration of pharmaceutical products in order to expedite and boost the growth of the Halal pharmaceutical industry for the benefit of the Ummah.

## 4. Tourism and Travel

Halal tourism has recently gained popularity, and is now fast becoming a new phenomenon in the general tourism industry. It refers to tourism products that provide hospitality services in accordance with Islamic beliefs and practices. This involves serving halal food, having separate swimming pools, spa and leisure activities for men and women, alcohol free dining areas, prayer facilities, and even women-only beach areas with Islamic swimming etiquette. Traditionally, halal tourism has been commonly associated with pilgrimages hajj and umrah. The growing affluent middle class Muslim consumers, and increase in the degree of interconnectivity which has made traveling a part and parcel of everyday life, are gradually changing the tourism preferences of Muslims from traditional destinations such as Mecca to top holiday destinations and resorts. With Muslim tourist's expenditure expected to rise to more than 13% of the entire global tourism expenditure by 2020, halal tourism has the potential to go mainstream and develop as an integral part of the burgeoning global halal market.(Dar, Azmi et al. 2013)

The halal tourism market represents 12.3% or USD126.1 billion of the total global outbound tourism market and is growing at 4.8% compared to the global average of 3.8%. In 2011 alone, Muslim travelers spent about USD126 billion.15 This figure is expected to reach USD419 billion by 2020. The MENA markets represent the largest share of the global Muslim tourist outbound expenditure at 60%.(Dar, Azmi et al. 2013)

Halal tourism has flourished in recent years to cater for the needs of Muslim travelers who want to enjoy full holiday services, which at the same time address their religious requirements as well as Islamic customs and culture. A number of countries have already adapted their tourism offers to include facilities and accommodations in accordance with the religious beliefs of Muslim tourists. Favorite destinations have predominantly been Islamic countries such as Malaysia, Turkey and Egypt. In recent years, non-Muslim countries including Australia, Singapore and France have shown strong interest in halal tourism. These destinations are favorite among Muslim travelers as they have halal certification bodies, which make it easier for tourists to find halal certified food outlets while vacationing there. Malaysia, for example, has been leading the way in the halal tourism industry, and has been successful in attracting Muslim tourists from all over the world, especially Middle Eastern travelers. Recently, Malaysia was ranked first among the top 10 halal friendly holiday destinations in the world. The ranking was based on several factors including availability of halal food, prayer facilities and halal friendly accommodation.

On the other hand, Muslim travelers have emerged as an attractive customer segment accounting for an estimated 11 percent of global outbound spend on travel and tourism in 2014, spending $142 billion in total. Comparatively this is a 6.3% increase from the 2013 Muslim travel expenditure that was $134 billion (updated based on adjusted methodology). Muslim outbound tourism expenditure is expected to grow to $233 billion market by 2020. In aggregate, the Muslim travel spending is third largest when compared to largest travel source countries — just after China ($160 billion) and the United States ($143 billion.) Top source countries of Muslim tourists based on 2014 expenditure were: Saudi Arabia ($17.8 billion), United Arab Emirates ($12.6 billion), Kuwait ($9.7 billion),

Qatar ($9.5 billion), Indonesia ($7.6 billion) and Iran ($7.5 billion). Regionally, Muslim Tourism expenditure was the highest in the following regions: MENA-GCC ($52 billion), MENA-Other ($21 billion) and East Asia ($19 billion) followed by Western Europe

($16 billion) and Central Asia ($10 billion). MENA-GCC represent 37% of the total Muslim travel spend even-though they are only 3% of the global Muslim population.(Thomson Reuters and Dinar Standard 2016)

The global beach resorts market is a high-growth market estimated at

$250 billion in 2014, representing 30 percent of the total hotel and resorts market, and with this share expected to grow going forward:(Salaam Gateway JANUARY 2016)

- The beach resorts landscape has broadened in scope, from primarily targeting price conscious travelers to addressing a diverse array of customer groups, and offering a wide range of price levels, from budget through to luxury.

- With Muslim travelers spending an estimated $28 billion on beach resorts in 2014, and with significant scope for further specialization in the industry, there has been a growing number of beach resorts primarily targeting Muslim travelers, and fully addressing Muslim lifestyle needs.

The report by Salaam Gateway has identified 32 Muslim-focused beach resorts in OIC countries addressing the broad range of lifestyle needs of Muslim travelers, as well as over 30 Muslim-friendly resorts:(Salaam Gateway JANUARY 2016)

- In addition to halal food, the absence of alcohol on premises and dedicated prayer spaces, all of these resorts attract Muslim families through providing segregated pools, fitness centers and beaches for women, and tend to compete on price, location and quality of service.
- Turkey is the most established market, with 28 resorts dedicated to Muslim travelers, and includes 3-, 4-, and 5-star resorts:

o 17 of these resorts offer peak-season family room prices below $300 per night of The remaining 11 have peak prices ranging from $300 up to $990 per night, with the most expensive being Angel's Marmaris 5-star resort, followed by Piynar Villa Hotel.

o The remaining Muslim-focused resorts are located in Egypt, Jordan, Kuwait, and UAE, with peak-season prices ranging from $264 up to $1,348 per night.

- 32 Muslim-friendly resorts were also identified, with 11 in Thailand and five in Maldives, which accommodate Muslim needs, including providing halal food, segregated leisure facilities for women, and offering alcohol-free premises .

**Tourism and Travel :Key Challenges and Opportunities Challenges**

↘↘ Accommodating both Muslims and non-Muslims at the same destination. This is especially relevant to beach destinations, where Muslims want to avoid gazing at bikini clad Westerners, while some non- Muslims prefer to party freely without being followed by watchful eyes. One approach to avoid this is designating separate areas for Muslims and others for non-Muslims. The Indonesian island, Lombok does precisely that. To avoid putting off non-Muslim visitors to Lombok, as well as avoid offending Muslim tourists by the skimpy outfits worn by sunbathers, the local government has identified areas that are suited to Muslim guests, where Western tourists need to cover up, whereas, party hotspots in the area, such as the tiny Gili Trawangan island off the West coast of Lombok remain unaffected.

↘↘ Marketing to Muslim travelers without alienating non-Muslims. Hotels and destinations that cater to Muslim tourists certainly do not want to attract the Muslim traveler segment at the expense of other markets, and therefore one dilemma is what their marketing strategy should be. One approach is to market themselves as a family-friendly hotel/destination without using the terms "Muslim" or "Halal". Al Jawhara, a Dubai-based hotel group is doing just that. In their ads, Jawhara promotes its "unique family oriented hospitality", despite the fact that the hotel clearly caters to Muslim needs. Another hotel group that successfully accommodates Muslim needs while being inclusive and not branding itself as a Halal hotel is Shaza Hotels. The luxury hotel operator focuses on authentic Arabian hospitality while being values-driven, and therefore appeals to both Muslims and non-Muslims alike.

Another way to avoid the dilemma of marketing to Muslims while non- alienating others, is to market to the Muslim audience through targeted marketing channels, such as Muslim media, local publications in Muslim majority countries, as well as targeted ad campaigns.

↘↘ Raising Financing. Some investors are still reluctant to invest in Muslim-friendly dry hotels and resorts as they fear there will be a loss of revenue in food and beverage. Laurent Voivenel of Hospitality Management Holdings believes that a dry hotel can yield the same profits as one that serves alcohol if the owners focus on banqueting.

↘↘ Being Muslim-friendly/Halal means different things to different people. The travel industry has not agreed on what the terms Halal Holiday or Muslim-friendly resort mean and each player is applying his or her own interpretation of the terms.

↘↘ An opportunity to develop Muslim-friendly resorts. There is a growing demand for Muslim friendly resorts. HalalBooking.com have been marketing Halal-friendly resorts in Turkey for the past 6 years. They started seeing bookings in the millions in 2014 per resort, and hope to reach 10 million per hotel for many of the hotels by the end of 2015 and in 2016. The popularity of these Halal friendly resorts has led the Antalya region, on the Southern coast of Turkey to add five new resorts in 2015, thereby increasing their total number of Halal-friendly resorts to fifteen. According to HalalBooking.com, the margins for all-inclusive Halal-friendly resorts are significantly higher than their mainstream counterparts, given that, alcohol,which is a high cost item, is taken away from the equation, resulting in millions of dollars in profit in one season for an all-inclusive resort. According to HalalBooking.com, more investors are becoming aware of the concept of Halal holidays, and they expect we will start seeing new hotels, resorts and villa complexes appearing in many more countries. An opportunity to target the rising middle class, especially in South East Asia. Many industry players are still targeting wealthy travellers from the GCC. While this makes sense for premium brands. There is a huge opportunity in developing mid-tier products for the mid-market segment. Mr. Laurent Voivenel of Hospitality Management Holdings believes that the long-term sustainability of the tourism industry depends on developing the budget sector that caters to the growing middle class.

↘↘ Opportunity to focus on themes such as voluntourism, eco- tourism, ethical tourism and experiential travel. Travel companies that cater to the Muslim market can differentiate themselves by providing themed trips that tie-in with the growing global tend towards ethical tourism and experiential travel, which are in-line with the teachings of Islam. One Muslim travel company that is involved in voluntourism and socially responsible travel is Holiday Bosnia. A Dubai-based company, Holiday Bosnia offers philanthropic trips to Bosnia in which travelers interact with the local community and may partake in charitable work, as well as donate to community projects.

At the end , Islamic tourism companies and operators should continue to improve and diversify their products and services, provide more attractive packages that respond to the needs of Muslims worldwide, including the Hajj, Umrah, heritage cites , trade and cultural exhibitions and recreation facilities. As one critic observed, Islamic tourism agencies should do better to present their products, local and International promotions. " They do not provide a strict timetable for tours, or if they do, it is not adhered to." Moreover , Governments and the general public everywhere should do their utmost to curb violence and terrorist activities, which paralyses everyday life and are especially damaging to the tourist industry. Government authorities are in the mean time advised to find appropriate strategies that avoid imposition of unnecessary travel restrictions and see Islamic tourism as a harbinger of better understanding among nations.(Kamali 2012)

## IV. The blockchain basis

Understanding blockchains is tricky. You need to understand their message before you can appreciate their potential. In addition to their technological capabilities, blockchains carry with them philosophical, cultural, and ideological underpinnings that must also be understood. Unless you're a software developer, blockchains are not a product that you just turn on, and use. Blockchains will enable other products that you will use, while you may not know there is a blockchain behind them, just as you do not know the complexities behind what you are currently accessing on the Web. Once you start to imagine the blockchains' possibilities on your own, without continuously thinking about trying to understand them at the same time, you will be in a different stage of your maturity for exploiting them. It is my belief that the knowledge transfer behind understanding the blockchain is easier than the knowledge about knowing where they will fit. It's like learning how to drive a car. I could teach you how to drive one, but cannot predict where you will take it. Only you know your particular business or situation, and only you will be able to figure out where blockchains fit, after you have learned what they can do. Of course, we will first go together on road tests and racing tracks to give you some ideas.(Mougayar, 2016)

In the simplest terms, a blockchain consists of a linked chain that stores auditable data in units called blocks. Many commentaries online start by explaining that a blockchain is similar to a Google document spreadsheet where multiple authors can contribute because of the mechanism of locking. Blockchain is a bit more complex than that example and has unique characteristics that make it an attractive technology for tagging, storing and tracking anything of value. Bitcoin was one of the first and most popular implementations of blockchain technology.

To begin, a blockchain consists of blocks, each block containing the data (anything of value), its own hash value (a unique cryptographic value containing characters and numbers generated through a complex computational algorithm) and a pointer to the hash of the previous block.(Sylvester, 2019)

The blockchain is part database, part development platform, part network enabler, so we need many instances of it and variations thereof. As an overlay on top of the Internet, blockchains can take many forms of implementations. Blockchains can be seen as a trust layer, an exchange medium, a secure pipe, a set of decentralized capabilities, and even more. That said, there are many analogies between the Web's early years and today's blockchain's evolution, in terms of how the technology will be adopted. Let us not forget that it took about three years for most companies to fully understand the Web's potential (1994–1997 roughly), after its initial commercialization, and it took seven years after the Internet's 1983 launch for the Web to come into play. There is no doubt the blockchain will remain a semi-mysterious, semi-complex phenomena for the period 2015–2018, just as it took Bitcoin three quiet years (2009–2012) before it became more visibly known to the general public. (Mougayar, 2016)

When Tim Berners-Lee created the first World Wide Web page in 1990, he wrote: "When we link information in the Web, we enable ourselves to discover facts, create ideas, buy and sell things, and forge new relationships at a speed and scale that was unimaginable in the analogue era."

In that short statement, Berners-Lee predicted search, publishing, e-commerce, e-mail, and social media, all at once, by a single stroke. The Bitcoin equivalent to that type of prescience by someone who just created something spectacular can be found in Satoshi Nakamato's 2008 paper, "Bitcoin: A Peer-to-Peer Electronic Cash System," arguably the root of modern blockchain-based cryptocurrency innovation.

The paper's abstract depicts Bitcoin's foundation, and it explains its first principles:(Mougayar, 2016)

- ✓ A purely *peer-to-peer* version of electronic cash would allow online payments to be sent *directly from one party to another without going through a financial institution*.
- ✓ A *trusted third party is not required* to prevent double-spending.
- ✓ We propose a *solution* to the double-spending problem *using a peer-to-peer network*.
- ✓ *The network timestamps transactions* by hashing them into an ongoing chain of hash-based proof-of-work, forming *a record that cannot be changed without redoing the proof-of-work*.
- ✓ The longest chain not only serves as proof of the sequence of events witnessed, but proof that it came from the largest pool of CPU power. As long as *a majority of CPU power is*

*controlled by nodes that are not cooperating to attack the network*, they'll generate the longest chain and outpace attackers.

- ✓ The network itself requires minimal structure. Messages are broadcast on a best-effort basis, and *nodes can leave and rejoin the network at will, accepting the longest proof-of-work chain as proof of what happened while they were gone.*

If you are a non-technical reader, and you focus on the italicized parts, you will start to get the gist of it. Please re-read the above points, until you have internalized Nakamoto's sequential logic! Seriously. You will need to believe and accept that validating peer-to-peer transactions is entirely possible by just letting the network perform a trust duty, without central interference or hand-holding.

Paraphrasing Nakamoto's paper, we should be left with these points:

- ✓ Peer-to-peer electronic transactions and interactions
- ✓ Without financial institutions
- ✓ Cryptographic proof instead of central trust
- ✓ Put trust in the network instead of in a central

institution

As it turns out, the "blockchain" is that technology invention behind Bitcoin, and what makes this possible. With Satoshi's abstract still in your mind, let us dive deeper with three different but complementary definitions of the blockchain: a technical, business, and legal one.

Technically, the blockchain is a back-end database that maintains a distributed ledger that can be inspected openly.

Business-wise, the blockchain is an exchange network for moving transactions, value, assets between peers, without the assistance of intermediaries.

The Web could not exist without the Internet. And blockchains could not be without the Internet. The Web made the Internet more useful, because people were more interested in using the information, than figuring out how to hook up computers together. Blockchain applications need the Internet, but they can bypass the Web, and give us another version that is more decentralized, and perhaps more equitable. That is one of the biggest promises of blockchain technology.

BLOCKCHAINS, LIKE THE WEB,
NEED THE INTERNET

There is more than one way to build blockchain applications. You can build them natively on a blockchain, or you could mix them in an existing Web application or "hybrid blockchain applications."(Mougayar, 2016)

FLAVORS OF BLOCKCHAIN APPLICATIONS

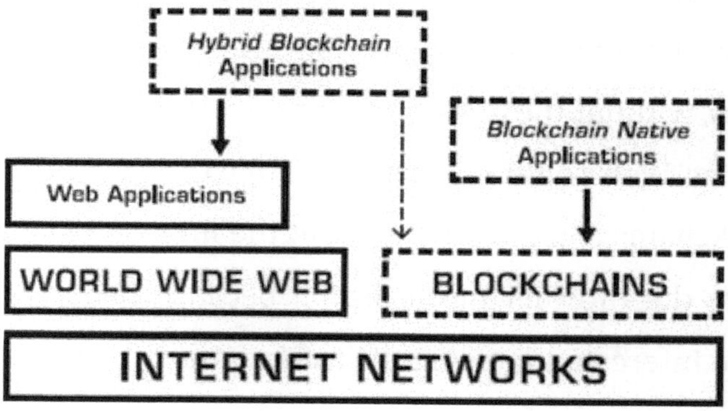


Types of Blockchain

Since the Internet is comprised of a public version and several private variations, blockchains will also follow that path. Therefore, we will have public and private blockchains. Some will be natively bolted to a blockchain, whereas others might be a hybrid implementation that is part of an existing Web or private application.(Mougayar, 2016)

Blockchains can be classified as public, private or hybrid variants, depending on their application:(Sultan, Ruhi, & Lakhani, 2018)

**Public** – Public blockchains have no single owner; are visible by anyone; their consensus process is open to all to participate in; and they are full decentralized. Bitcoin is an example of a public blockchain.

Public blockchain is open source in which anyone can participate, without the need of permission. On such platform, anyone can download the code or software, and start running a full node on the local device, validating transactions in the network, thus participating in the consensus process. Due to the public nature, anyone can see or audit transaction on the public block explorer; however, the parties of a transaction remain anonymous. There are few advantages of using public blockchain. It has a potential to disrupt current business models through disintermediation. Moreover, there is no need to maintain servers or system admins by the central authority, this radically reduces the cost of creating and running decentralized applications

(DApps). Some examples of public blockchain are Bitcoin, Ethereum, and Litecoin.(Abojeib & Habib, 2019)

**Private** – (also called permissioned) Private blockchains use privileges to control who can read from and write to the blockchain. Consensus algorithms and mining usually aren't required as a single entity has ownership and controls block creation.

Private blockchain can be defined as a platform controlled by a single or centralized organization with restricted number of nodes within that organization. It is valuable for solving efficiency, security and fraud problems within traditional institutions, but the most important feature of decentralization is not available for private blockchain. It has same advantages as of the consortium blockchain, but it is different from it in the sense that it has more restriction and is not distributed.(Abojeib & Habib, 2019)

**Hybrid** – Also known as consortium, these blockchains are public only to a privileged group. The consensus process is controlled by known, privileged servers using a set of rules agreed to by all parties. Copies of the blockchain are only distributed among entitled participants; the network is therefore only partly decentralized.

It is also called federated blockchain. It operates under the control of a specific group of organizations which are allowed to perform the role of full nodes. As opposed to public blockchain, the structure does not give access to all persons to participate in the process of verifying transactions. The consensus process is controlled by a preselected set of nodes in which the protocol defines the minimum number required to sign every block in order for the block to be valid. The right to read the blockchain can either be public or restricted to the participants only. This type of blockchain has some specific advantages. For example, it reduces transaction costs; avoids data redundancies; and replaces legacy systems. It is also helpful for simplifying document handling and getting rid of semi manual compliance mechanisms. The transaction processing in such blockchain is faster than a public blockchain, which means there is a potential for higher scalability. It also provides more privacy, but at the cost of lesser transparency. Consortium blockchain can be suitable for the traditional banking sector. Some of the examples are: R3 Corda (for banks); EWF (for energy), B3i (for insurance).(Abojeib & Habib, 2019)

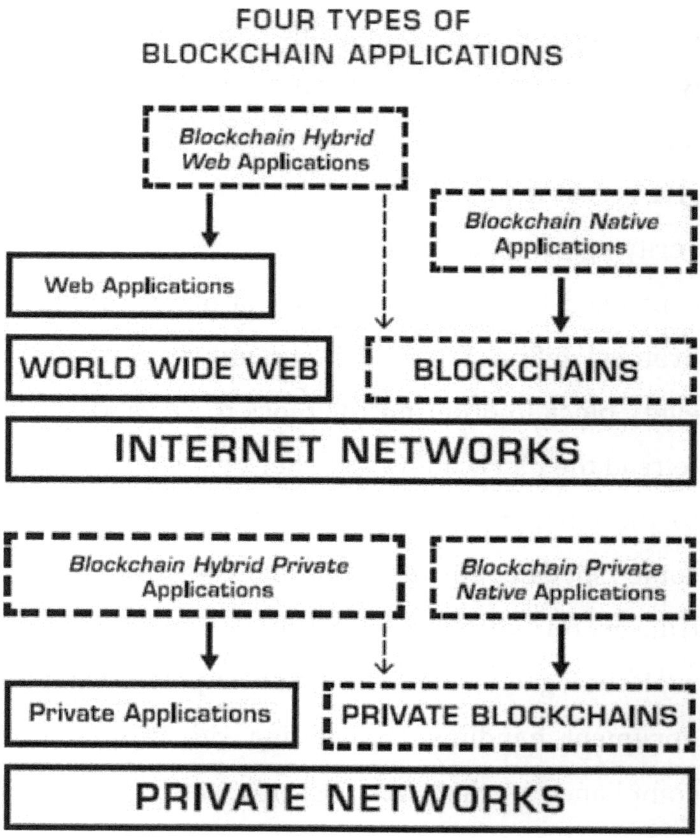


### Investments in Blockchain

Major firms across the financial services landscape have made investments in blockchain-based start-ups, continuing into 2018. The herd of new strategic investors is playing an increasingly important role in the health of the financing market for these start-ups. While quarterly deal activity dropped to its lowest point since Q2'14 in Q4'16, the quarter's top two financing deals featured investments by major corporate and financial services players. More specifically, distributed ledger developer Axoni saw Wells Fargo lead its US$18M Series A offering, which included JP Morgan, Goldman Sachs,F-Prime Capital, and Thomson Reuters as investors. As Axoni CEO Greg Schvey said, "Deploying distributed ledger technology in production at this scale is a watershed moment for the industry. The combination of technology and business expertise being contributed to this project from across the participating firms is unparalleled and the benefits are clear." Among the financial services investors are insurance providers such as TransAmerica, New York Life, and Mitsui Sumitomo Insurance Group (MSIG); payments giants including Visa, MasterCard, and American Express; as well as banks like Mitsubishi UFJ Financial Group (MUFG), Citi, Santander, and Canadian Imperial Bank of Commerce (CIBC). Strategic investment into bitcoin or blockchain start-ups over the past three years hit its apex in the fall of 2015 and into the winter of 2016. In recent months, Deloitte, Miami International Holdings (MIAX), and Credit China placed their first blockchain bets, with Deloitte taking a corporate minority stake in appropriately named blockchain settlement and payments platform SETL. In total, over fifty financial services firms or their strategic investment arms have invested in a bitcoin or blockchain-specific start-ups since the start of 2014. Of note, a relatively small number of start-ups have captured most financial services investments in the bitcoin and blockchain space. For example, the seven firms listed below—Circle Internet Financial, Coinbase, Ripple, BitFury Group, Blockstream, Digital Asset Holdings, and Chain—have received nearly US$625M in funding and are all listed among the top ten most well-funded bitcoin and blockchain companies. Between Circle's Series E round of US$110 million, US$118 million raised by Orbs, a purported "consumer-ready blockchain" service, US$75 million Series B round for Paris-based secure hardware wallet-maker Ledger, they account for a significant number of financial services investors. As of the first half of 2018, the total investments in blockchain-related companies have exceeded US$1.3 billion across all investment rounds worldwide. Reported dollar volume invested in VC rounds raised by blockchain companies surpassed totals in 2017.(Mohamed & Ali, 2018)

There are many indications that blockchain is fundamentally altering the business landscape. Here are just a few significant shifts:

**Tokenization** — the representation of real or virtual assets on a blockchain — is spreading to raw materials, finished goods, income-producing securities, membership rights and more. You can now represent on a blockchain almost everything businesses do.

**Initial coin offerings (ICOs)**, in which a company sells a predefined number of digital tokens to the public, are funneling billions of dollars into blockchain platforms. Increasingly an alternative to classic debt/capital funding as provided today by venture capital and private equity firms and banks, ICOs in the first five months of 2018 raised $13.7 billion. The largest ICOs to date have been diverse and included EOS, which is focused on blockchain infrastructure; Huobi Token, a coin for a South Korean crypto exchange; and Hdac, an Internet of Things platform.

**Enterprise software platforms** that are the engine for company operations such as finance, human resources and customer relationship management are beginning to integrate blockchain. For example, Microsoft, Oracle, SAP and Salesforce have all announced blockchain initiatives. In the future, many core business processes will run on — or interoperate with — blockchain-based systems. Using blockchain in concert with enterprise resource planning platforms will enable companies to streamline processes, facilitate data sharing and improve data integrity.

**New industry and territory leaders** are emerging. Gartner has found that 82% of reported blockchain use cases were in financial services in 2017, but that sector's portion dropped to 46% of reported use cases in 2018. The survey respondents still perceive financial services to be the current and near-term future leader of blockchain, but also see potential in industrial products, energy and utilities and healthcare. Moreover, an early center of gravity in the US and Europe is shifting. The survey respondents believe that the US is the most advanced territory in developing blockchain today, but that in three to five years, the leader will be China.

According to PwC[1], the financial sector stands to gain the most from blockchain-based service

[1] https://www.pwc.com/blockchainsurvey

implementations, followed by industrial products and the manufacturing sector, energy and utilities and then the healthcare sector.

Nevertheless, a PwC survey of about 600 blockchain-savvy executives revealed that the biggest barrier to blockchain adoption was regulatory uncertainty. Interoperability and the potential failure of different blockchains to work together were identified as major challenges.

Building a blockchain becomes more complex when third parties participate. Consider a multinational that builds a blockchain to manage an intercompany process such as transfer pricing or treasury management. Historically, the company might be struggling with dozens of ERP systems and inconsistent data and processes. Instead of one central ledger for each subsidiary, a single distributed ledger can eliminate the need for reconciliation. Companies are exploring how they might use internal digital tokens to represent cash or other assets, with the aim of streamlining their movement between business units. Instead of time-consuming (and costly) bank transfers, currency conversions and multiple emails about each transaction, a tokenized transfer can be conducted in near real time via smart contracts and allow users to track each transaction's progress.

A company creating a blockchain for itself will undoubtedly confront challenges related to internal buy-in, data harmonization and scale. Still, this company can set and enforce the rules of the blockchain, just as it does with its ERP today. But generally speaking, you don't realize the greatest return on investment in blockchain if you're building it just for yourself. Blockchain's benefits are best realized when different industry participants come together to create a shared platform. Of course, when you start inviting third parties to engage, you can't write the rules yourself.

PwC survey respondents echo these concerns, with regulatory uncertainty (48%), lack of trust among users (45%) and the ability to bring the network together (44%) making up the top barriers to blockchain adoption.

Blockchain, by its very definition, should engender trust. But in reality, companies confront trust issues at nearly every turn. For one, users must build confidence in the technology itself. As with any emerging technology, challenges and doubts exist around blockchain's reliability, speed, security and scalability.

And there are concerns regarding a lack of standardization and the potential lack of interoperability with other blockchains.

Also contributing to the blockchain trust gap is a lack of understanding. Even now, many executives are unclear on what blockchain really is and how it is changing all facets of business. Although the public narrative has moved beyond bitcoin, even the more recent focus and hype around ICOs only hint at the potential impact. Blockchain's role as a dual-pronged change agent — as a new form of infrastructure and as a new way to digitize assets through tokens, including cryptocurrency — is not easy to explain. Think about other new technologies: users can try on virtual reality goggles or watch a drone take flight. But blockchain is abstract, technical and happening behind the scenes.

Another challenge for blockchain is building trust in the network. It is perhaps ironic that a technology meant to bring consensus hits a stumbling block on the early need to design rules and standards. Take payment systems and mechanisms in banking. Though everyone plays by the rules of existing systems today, they don't necessarily agree on how an alternative blockchain-based model should be designed and operated.

Likewise, there's a lack of comfort regarding regulation. The majority of regulators are still coming to terms with blockchain and cryptocurrency. Many territories have begun studying and discussing the issues, particularly as they relate to financial services, but the overall regulatory environment remains unsettled.

It is perhaps ironic that a technology meant to bring consensus hits a stumbling block on the early need to design rules and standards.

Based on the properties of the blockchain and its characteristic as being a generic data store for all kinds of data, we can come up with the following generic use cases:(Drescher, 2017)

**Proof of Existence**

This use of the blockchain focuses on storing data for the sole purpose of proving its existence. Hence, this use utilizes neither the ordering nor the time-stamping capabilities of the blockchain. Concrete applications are, for example, registries of items that are supposed to be unique such as brand names, patents, license codes, and Internet or e-mail addresses.

**Proof of Nonexistence**

This use of the blockchain focuses on the opposite of the proof of existence. It provides ways to verify whether specific entries or items do not exist in the blockchain. Concrete applications of this could be records of complaints, fines, or convictions.

**Proof of Time**

In this case not only the sheer existence of an entry in the blockchain is important but also the time when the entry was added. The blockchain can serve that need since the blocks of the blockchain-data-structure store the time when the process of adding them was started. Applications that benefit from the time-stamping capabilities of the blockchain are those that track the occurrence of events in time such as delivery or notification tracking, tracking of payments, tracking of orderly opening and closing of public bidding procedures, and management of predictions.

**Proof of Order**

This pattern of usage utilizes the ordering capability of the blockchain. Applications that benefits from that property of the blockchain are those that track the relative ordering of events regardless of their absolute time, for example, tracking of application processes, auditing public bidding procedures, and escrow services. Proving that some event was the first or the last of its kind is a specific example of proof of order. This kind of proof can be important when resources are allocated in the same order in which certain claims or documents are submitted such as college or university applications, patent applications, or copyright claims.

**Proof of Identity**

Proof of identity can be considered a specific case of

proof of existence because it proves that a certain identity already exists. The blockchain serves that use case since it not only stores data that can be used to identify someone or something but also provides basic security concepts for identification and authentication. Concrete applications of this use pattern are digital identity

documents for people, animals, or goods. Governments could utilize such blockchains as part of their e-government strategy for managing personal documents, drivers' licenses, or passports.

**Proof of Authorship**

This use pattern focuses on proving that a specific person or institution added certain data to the blockchain. The blockchain can serve that purpose because it not only stores data that can be identified by its cryptographic fingerprint but also offers basic security concepts such as identification, authentication, and authorization. Identification and authentication are necessary to identify authors and verify their identity. Authorization is necessary in this use case in order to prevent someone from adding data to the blockchain without having the right to do so. Applications that utilize this use pattern are, for example, electronic publishing, tracking of content changes in documents, content delivery, collaborative editing, and protecting copyrights.

**Proof of Ownership**

This use pattern focuses on managing and clarifies ownership. It relies on all previously mentioned patterns such as proof of existence, proof of order, proof of identity, and proof of authorship together with the three basic security concepts: identification, authentication, and authorization. Applications that utilize this use pattern are, for example, systems for managing ownership of real estate, cars, company shares, bonds, digital money, or cryptographic currencies.

**Specific Use Cases**

The blockchain is agnostic with respect to the data it stores. Hence, the range of data being stored in the blockchain and the range of its application areas are as wide and as diverse as human activities themselves. As a result, it is impossible to provide a complete overview of all blockchain applications. For that reason, this section presents a small selection of concrete blockchain application areas in which the blockchain is already used or may be used soon:(Drescher, 2017)

- *Payments*: Managing ownership and transfer of digital fiat currencies.
- *Cryptocurrencies*: Managing ownership and creation of digital instruments of payment that exist independently from any government, central bank, or other central institution.
- *Micropayments*: Transfer of small amounts of money that would be too costly by using traditional means of transfer.
- *Digital assets*: Managing creation, ownership, and transfer of digital items that have value in their own right or represent valuable goods in the real world.
- *Digital identity*: Proving identity and authentication based on unique digital items.
- *Notary services*: Digitizing, storing, and verifying documents or contracts and proof of ownership or transfer.
- *Compliance and audit*: Auditing business activities of people or organizations in regulated industries in an audit track.
- *Tax*: Calculating and collecting taxes based on transactions or on sole ownership, reducing tax avoidance, or double taxation.
- *Voting*: Creating, distributing, and counting digital

ballot papers.

- *Record management*: Creation and storing of medical records.

## Blockchain in Halal Supply Chains

Two fundamental concepts in the Islamic worldview that would have significant implications on economic (including financial) behaviors are the concept of man as khalifah (vicegerent) and 'abd (servant/slave). The Qur´an (Surah al-Baqarah,Qur'an 2:30) mentions that the human being has been created to be a khalifah, a vicegerent on earth to establish God's commandments, a unique position (with a mission) not granted to other creations. To be a khalifah, the human being is endowed with a delegation of authority from God to fulfill "consciously" (not by force) the divine patterns on earth. He is granted free will to either implement or annihilate these divine patterns through his actions. He is the only being that can act contrary to his nature (i.e., not fulfilling God's primordial command), while no other creations be it animals, plants, or angels can do so. Human beings are free to use the bounties and blessings conferred upon them (taskhir), but at the same time, they must carry out their duty toward God mainly as an 'abd (who serve and worship Him) and khalifah (who holds amanah as God's representative on the earth) to isti'mar, that is, to prosper the earth and to create a moral social order on earth. All man's actions, including his economic activities, should be viewed in this complete commitment to God by obeying the prescribed framework. Another example that shapes the relationship of the ethical concepts that make up the ethical foundation of Islam is the belief of the connection of dunya (the present world) and akhirah (the hereafter). Muslims are advised to be very conscious of this correlation in every action they take and choices they make. When all economic goals are only directed to the happiness of human beings in this world, institutions are likely to suffer from immoral sentiments that are opposed to upholding divine laws meant to benefit human beings. In conventional economics, a rational individual is free to maximize his utility as much as possible without any moral, social, or religious commitment. Consideration for a "hereafter" reward and punishment of the consequences of economic choices and decisions made are not included in such a theory. Instead, an Islamic or more enlightened or universal concept of justice and responsible viceregency would constrain an individual maximization of utility in view of the greater good. The presence of al-jannah (Heaven) and al-jahannam (Hell) provides "the form of the moral conscience" whenever a man chooses to do anything in this world. It is the very source of moral values. Man, as long as he lives as a member of the Muslim community, is morally required to always make choices that are connected with good and to avoid those that are connected with harm. In fact, these universal principles also apply to all other religions and value systems. However, behavioral economics informs us that our choices are also governed by our emotions as well as situational factors and the environment. Even with deep moral precepts, our actions are highly influenced by our moods, feelings, and peer pressure, which may be irrational to moral decision making. As such, if the prescribed behaviors of the Economic Man can be mechanized in a system that uses technology to overcome our irrationality, those behaviors that harm the integrity of the financial system in the long run can be prevented. Technological advancement may have the ability to limit4 poor decisions and detect and prevent fraud and deception early before a collapse in trust and confidence occurs again.(Mohamed & Ali, 2018)

The maqasid has an important aspect to developing Islamic economics which is maslahah or public interest. Money in Islam performs a "social-role," that is why the main goals of Islamic finance are to distribute wealth efficiently, promoting socio-economy justice, and ensure the prosperity and well-being for all. Meanwhile, the gap in financing for SDGs is currently estimated at $ 2.5 trillion every year. According to Thomson Reuters' projections, Islamic finance assets are projected to grow to $3.2 trillion by 2020. It depicts Islamic finance potentials to support the SDGs by providing innovative financing solutions. Compared to individual contribution, giving zakat or sadaqah through formal institutions, investing in Islamic bonds, can increase outreach, targeting the people in need, and providing a more strategic and sustainable solution. However, there are several challenges, inefficiency, a lack of transparency in terms of how the funds are collected, managed, distributed, and the differing views of Islamic scholars on how these should be dealt with the rulings or fatwa.[2]

In Islam, man is entrusted with an amanah (trust) to establish responsibility on earth by means of virtues and

---

[2]Gratiyana Ningrat ,Islamic finance and blockchain: Can it bring greater impact? In: https://www.thejakartapost.com/academia/2018/11/24/islamic-finance-and-blockchain-can-it-bring-greater-impact.html

bounties endowed to him by God, his initiative, creativity,and labor (isti'mar). Nature has been created for human beings but man is also required to establish a moral social order on earth. The concept of amanah implies that in all his actions, man should choose to prosper the earth (islah) by making the best use of resources and to fully utilize the virtues inherent in him to isti'mar the earth. Ifsad (fasad) or adversity or corruption, is to be avoided in managing one's role as a khalifah. Being a khalifah, man has also been granted authority to freely manage nature/universe and to cooperate with his fellow beings to complete the task of khalifah. As our world and the economy evolves, we seek new ways (innovate) to cope with the challenge's evolution brings. We believe technology is a great way to do this, and the main building block to enable trust in impersonal financial transactions in a highly globalized environment can be identified as blockchain. This innovation that will shape the future will not only play a crucial role in boosting the financial sector (banking, takaful, investment, etc.) including the Islamic finance sector but also other economic transactions that will characterize the sharing economy. Religious tenets, in general, could be viewed as the force behind the "invisible hand" that Adam Smith had probably alluded to, where in the pursuit of self-interest, the "invisible hand" will safeguard the collective interest. There always has been a moral and ethical obligation to pursuing one's own interest because we do not live in isolation. If we choose to ignore these obligations, the unspoken social contract breaks down and it would lead to the tragedy of commons. Building trust by upholding ethical and moral obligations, hence, reinforces public civility and communal solidarity, removes fears and mistrust in public and private institutions for a harmonious and profitable existence, by reducing risk in highly uncertain times through shared goals and reciprocal undertaking. And as we will see in the next few sections, specific technology, like blockchain, will be a key enabler to further encourage this and play a significant role in the new sharing economy.(Mohamed & Ali, 2018)

The blockchain in Islamic finance and banking will surely help the Islamic banks, and financial institutes to succeed. Without worry about the interest and other such issues Islamic banking system will be able to work more productively. Management of loans and other relatable services will become easy. in addition to reducing fraud and risk, it can bring down the high costs associated with Islamic finance. The cost of processing Islamic financial products is higher than regular financial services products, so blockchain is a very effective tool to bring down the cost in the back-end processing systems of Islamic finance companies The real challenge, going forward, will be the legality of smart contracts, and the global regulatory framework needed to establish true peer-to-peer lending across borders; just because it is legal in one country, does not make it so in the next.

However, the power and potential of blockchain and smart contracts is being recognized across the business and political spectrum. While it may take regulators some time to catch up, broader adoption will lead to sensible regulation.

Is Islamic finance and Blockchain are fully compatible with each other?. The answer is: a definite possibility with a caveat - by defining the appropriate behavior. Off course, the question is NOT about whether the existing bitcoins and cryptocurrencies are permissible under the Islamic Shari'a. This issue is left for the Islamic scholars to come with the appropriate answer (and for that matter, is NOT the paramount issue that we should be focused on). The most important features of Blockchain is about: a) It is a PEER-TO-PEER system of transactions; b) It is based on fully DISTRIBUTED system; and c) It is an AUTONOMOUS process (AI). Islamic finance is about enforcing righteous behavior, and blockchain is about "coding" those behaviors onto a full system of AI, which would then ensure that those behaviors are adhered to autonomously, without further interference of another party. It then becomes "self-enforcing", "self-regulating", "self-correcting", and "self-performing" platform. If all the statement above are true, then the answer of "a definite possibility" would be true. (Hasni bin Wan Sulaiman, 2017)

There are various interesting applications of blockchain in halal supply chains that can bring different benefits:

Globally, there are almost 2 billion of Muslims from the 7.6 billion people in the world. Due to religious reasons, this enormous market of Muslims consciously seeks trusted, halal certified sources for their food, cosmetics, home care, pharmaceuticals, daily products and Shariah complied products to invest in. According to statistics, the global Halal market value that is recorded at approximately 1.4 trillion USD in 2017 is expected to reach 2.6 trillion USD in 2023.

Blockchain – with its characteristic that is high in transparency and traceability will be a good solution in providing reliable data and increase trust in the halal supply chains; increase seamless and efficient halal process from source to point of consumer purchase; improve sustainability of halal supply chains; and increase consumer's confidence in halal brands; and global recognition of halal products. Halal blockchains provide clear advantages for manufacturers, brand owners, retailers, logistics service providers, distributors, and halal certification bodies for better trust and authenticity.

The food industry is where trust is key to its operations. From farmers and producers to kitchens and end consumers, every step in the food industry can be improved by blockchain technology. A distributed ledger enables users to keep track of food origins, traceability, and quality control of food along the entire supply chain. As a system that can integrate data from all stakeholders into the ledger, blockchain technology can greatly benefit the food industry. However, some supply chains require even more transparency and traceability, and one of the areas that can make use of blockchain technology is the global halal market. Halal — which refers to the way that food should be produced and prepared according to Islamic law — is the food standard to which Muslims worldwide adhere. Moreover, halal food is considered to be healthier and more sustainable for the food industry. In recent years, with the rise in popularity of halal food, many producers that do not meet halal standards and requirements have been attempting to pass their food products as halal.[3]

A technology that can step in to alleviate this issue is blockchain, which can offer a transparent way to keep track of where food comes from, its producers, and relevant data which can vouch for the authenticity of halal food in the supply chain. Using this technology to guarantee halal standards, blockchain will open opportunities for new players in the market to offer their halal products to consumers all over the world. The food industry is set to undergo huge changes once the digital transformation to blockchain is implemented. This new technology will change the halal food market in numerous ways, from ensuring that all information

---

[3] Global Halal Market Turns to Blockchain for Supply Chain Integrity, https://www.asiablockchainreview.com/global-halal-market-turns-to-blockchain-for-supply-chain-integrity/

about halal food, from its origin, quality assurances, to supply chain journey may be gathered into a distributed ledger that is transparent to all stakeholders. Whether it is the name of the butcher, the logistics company, the supermarket or the restaurant, all data about halal food can be gathered in the blockchain, enabling a flow of communication and overall greater trust in the quality of halal food that reaches consumers. For end consumers, blockchain technology will allow them to check the information of halal food using an application or website that may be accessed from anyone's smartphone.

Blockchain-based technologies, once implemented, are expected to be able to generate many more solutions for the $1.4 trillion global halal food industry. Halal food is unique compared to other types of food, as its religious laws state that halal food must be prepared and processed in certain ways, and must not ever contain any pork. Though globally-recognized labels such as HACCP (Hazard Analysis and Critical Control Points), GMP (Good Manufacturing Practice), and GHP (Good Hygiene Practice) have all been used in the halal food system to ensure that food is appropriately handled, blockchain technology can integrate all relevant information and gather them in a distributed ledger that may be made available to all stakeholders. There are numerous requirements for halal food that blockchain technology can be used to address. At the farm, the animal will receive an identification number, which can be stored in the ledger to monitor its food intake and living conditions. Then at the butcher, all documents relating to the animal's health and various timestamps can be added to the blockchain, in order to determine the cut of meat from the animal, the manner in which the meat was processed, and to verify that the meat is halal, according to religious laws. In the system, to ensure that halal meat is up to standards, the meat can also be tested with a DNA sensor after it is processed, then monitored with smart packaging that can track the logistics of the product from factory to supermarket or restaurant.

The sensors, as well as smart packaging in the supply chain, can also be developed to immediately send information to the blockchain to keep track of the halal product. Moreover, environmental data from locations to custom controls can also be stored in the blockchain system.

A large discussion group on halal blockchains was held with the captains of industry on 15 May 2017 at

Universiti Malaysia Pahang in Kuantan (Malaysia) organized by the Faculty of Industrial Management. This large discussion group showed that halal supply chains have inherent problems or flaws, namely in (1) traceability (ability to verify the location of a product) and organizing product recalls; (2) transportation and warehousing (storage) compliance downstream the supply chain in accordance to halal requirements; (3) end-to-end chain integrity (unbroken chain): from source to point of consumer purchase; (4) different halal systems and interpretations of different markets; and (5) lack of integration of information technology systems. These problems require a radically different approach to how halal supply chains are orchestrated. Halal blockchains have the potential to solve all of the above halal industry problems! (Tieman & Darun, 2017)

Blockchain is already called the fourth industrial revolution. It is a digital public ledger containing stringed data blocks with information, similar to our DNA.[4] It is not stored somewhere centrally, but distributed on many servers throughout the world.

---

[4] Halal blockchain to boost supply chain transparency, May 29, 2017 . at : http://halalsupplychainmanagement.blogspot.com/2017/05/halal-blockchain-to-boost-supply-chain.html

Blockchains are encrypted and automatically synchronized in the distributed blockchains and makes them a trusted public ledger that everyone can inspect, but no single user controls. A halal blockchain is a digital ledger of all halal supply chain transactions that have ever been executed. It is constantly growing as 'completed' blocks are added to it with a new set of recordings. The blocks are added to the blockchain in a linear, chronological order. Each node in the halal supply chain network gets a copy of the blockchain, which gets downloaded automatically upon joining the halal supply chain network. The halal blockchain has complete information about the addresses and their supply chain path right from source to the point of consumer purchase. As the halal blockchain database is shared by all nodes participating in a halal supply chain network, information is easily verified by just scanning the QR-code (a two-dimensional barcode) on a product. Blockchains pre-program the halal requirement for the destination market, halal storage-transportation-terminal handling terms, coding of halal on freight documents, and many more. In a blockchain you can easily identify the parties that committed fraud, as this remains visible. This discourages the industry to commit fraud in halal supply chains. Halal blockchains provide clear advantages for manufacturers, brand owners, retailers, logistics service providers, distributors, and halal certification bodies. For a better trust and authenticity of country's halal brands, halal certification bodies should embrace this new technology to support the halal industry in case of a halal issue, or worse, a halal crisis. They should support the halal certification of logistics service providers, distributors and retailers in order to facilitate a higher compliance in transportation and warehousing downstream the supply chain. Harmonization and standardization of halal supply chain standards in different jurisdictions are essential in the coming years to better support halal industries and their global supply chains.(Sadouskaya, 2017; Tieman & Darun, 2017)

At the same time it allows rating of halal logistics service providers based on the performance of their services. Robust, effective, and efficient halal supply chains are only possible with more intensive collaboration between companies in the supply chain. Blockchain technology allows halal networks to better use available halal assets, like halal warehouses & distribution centers, halal transport & containers, and halal compliant sea & air terminals. At this moment we see that brand owners have difficulty in dealing with halal issues and a halal crisis, as they are highly dependent on the speed of the halal certification body to verify possible claims of a halal integrity breach. As this verification might take a week, the damage is already done. Blockchains allow for instant verification in a transparent way and effective isolation of the issue. Blockchain technology enhances information sharing in the secured situation through the entire supply chain. The data stored on the public blockchain is accessible to everyone and cannot be tampered with. Therefore, it increases the trust, security and transparency in halal supply chain (Tan, Yan, Chen, & Liu, 2018)

With all data stored in the distributed ledger, it is available to all stakeholders, including the consumer who can access the information through a website or mobile application. For governments, blockchain can offer solutions regarding import controls of halal products, which will raise the standards of regulatory compliance.

Once information is sent to the blockchain from the different suppliers along the supply chain, it may be monitored for other purposes, such as legal and tax purposes. Businesses can also benefit from blockchain technology, as both B2B (Business to Business) and B2C (Business to Consumer) relations will be enhanced with greater transparency and assurance of authenticity. Consumers of halal food will be more confident that with just a QR code that can be scanned using mobile applications, they will be able to trace the origins and manner of production of the food product. Ultimately, blockchain technology can offer a platform for all players in the halal food supply chain to demonstrate their transparency and responsibility for their products. With the halal market's continuous growth, blockchain can offer a better solution that will ensure more high-quality halal products for all consumers.[5]

what about its application in the Muslim world or more directly in the Halal economy? Figure below, adapting the principal agent framework in for the interaction between a Halal food manufacturer who needs to establish trust in its product by securing a Halal logo (from the Halal ministry/government body). We

[5] Halal blockchain to boost supply chain transparency, May 29, 2017 . at : http://halalsupplychainmanagement.blogspot.com/2017/05/halal-blockchain-to-boost-supply-chain.html

are depicting the various parties involved before the Halal retail buyer (HRB) who ultimately purchases a food product. Across the chain of interactions there are various contractual obligations before the HRB makes a purchase which is driven by only one factor: the Halal logo, the trusted logo. The HRB is making an inherent assumption that all the contractual fulfillment has happened. (Rana & Akinlaso, Q3 2018)

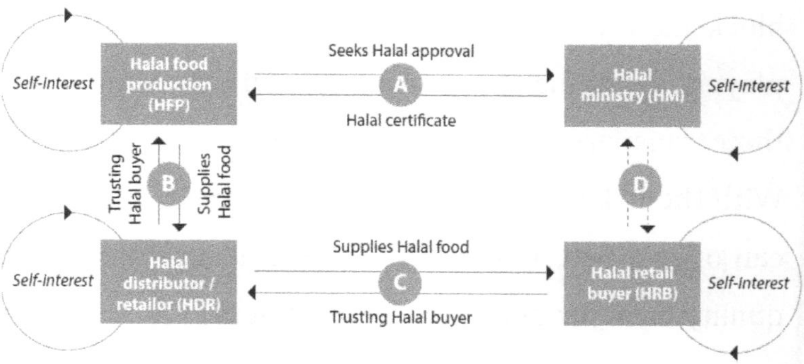


*Principal-agent interactions for Halal food*

*A. HFP needs a bona fi de unadulterated approval from HM; HM*

*need to deliver an authentication stamp saying Halal to HP.*

*B. HFP distributes Halal products to HDR; HDR pays HP*

*C. HDR provides Halal Products to HRBs*

*D. HRBs have bona fi de feelings that Halal stamp is authentic*

*Moral hazard: The entire value chain reeks of moral hazard problems due to self-interest. Perhaps the only entity relying on a bona fide response is the end buyer who is likely making a purely unadulterated decision purely based on trust via the actual Halal logo.*

Use case: Blockchain in Halal food sector

Is blockchain the silver bullet to all problems that might exist in the sector? How does blockchain solve this problem? Consider Figure below where a potential blockchain solution is depicted to address the problem of information asymmetry. It does so by allowing the end buyer to verify that the entire value chain is compliant with Islamic requirements and limits the amount of potential fraud. Let's say a producer has completed the manufacturing process for the Halal food, say beef, and is now ready to deliver to the market. Before the physical transaction or shipping of the product, the manufacturer will perform certain Halal compliance and authentication measures (ie Halalticate) as part of the due diligence.(Rana & Akinlaso, Q3 2018)

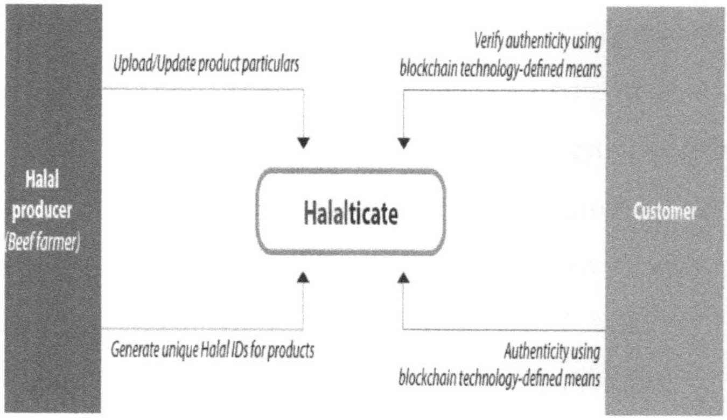


Blockchain model

Only after such due diligence will the product be eligible for the Halal logo, which is a mark of trust signaling to the retail consumer that the product is good and ready for consumption.

However, the process is still tainted with smidges of information asymmetry and risks, which leaves the consumer in doubts if not dismayed. Such risks can be managed by adopting either of the two methods presented in the principal-agent framework: screening and signaling.

Applying the screening method allows the consumer to verify the products authenticity in such a way that guarantee Genuity and satisfaction. This is where the blockchain technology comes in handy as it presents the possibility of a detailed trail of the beef and enables anyone to trace the

movement of the beef, right from its grazing ranch to the abattoir and down to the retail seller.

Signaling comes from the producer – the critical signal being that they have the food certify ed via the appropriate HM. Again, blockchain technology comes very suitable in securing and preserving such signals, making them tamperproof for the general public. Combining both method in a single platform and powering its application using blockchain technology will provide the trust needed in the transaction and eliminate the information asymmetry problem and its associated risk.

Consider a simple illustration below:(Rana & Akinlaso, Q3 2018)

1. The Halal food manufacturer uploads product particulars alongside certify cation from respective issuing authority to a blockchain platform, Halalticate;

2. The platform registers the product, and generates an immutable digital footprint using the product's description and Halal particulars in its blockchain database. The digital footprints will be in form of Unique IDs in various forms (Alphanumeric code, along with secure pattern, QR code, bar code or short links) for an

individual product, batch or category;

3. Manufacturer attaches the Unique IDs to the product label and starts shipment.

On the other hand, the Halal customer who is about to purchase the product would verify the authenticity of the product in the following steps:(Rana & Akinlaso, Q3 2018)

1. The customer looks up the product's unique (Halal) IDs;

2. Customer sends at least one of the unique IDs to the Halalticate platform for verify cation using a mobile device via SMS, QR scan or NFC facility;

3. The customer receives an instant report and audit trail on the product (with detailed product description and Halal particulars).

## V. The Challenges of Developing the Halal Industry

It would be no exaggeration to say that Europe today faces enormous upheavals. Not a day goes by in the power-centers of Berlin, Paris and London without new anxieties emerging around indebted states and urgently-needed plans for yet more rescue packages. What is at stake is the future role of nation-states in the European Union, and of course the prosperity of a whole continent. The biggest financial and debt crisis in human history has reached the heart of European societies, and it has made them deeply insecure.

After a decade of the so-called war against terror it is once again clear that we live in an age dominated by economic issues. Economic power has knocked politics off the pedestal of its primacy and the possibility of acquiring vast quantities of capital dominates the political landscape. It is not extremists, however regrettable their existence may be, who are undermining and endangering our democracies, it is economic conditions.

In all of this there are two areas in which the elites of Europe remain dangerously uninformed. For many years they have failed to notice the relentless pressure exerted by the instruments of modern financial technology, and the dangers these instruments bring. Until recently only a very few specialists inside European politics knew what a derivative was. Parliamentarians complain publicly that they fundamentally do not understand the things being done to save the euro.

Secondly, aside from a sprinkling of catchphrases, Islam in Europe remains an unknown quantity. Discussion about Muslims in Europe usually deals only with the various manifestations of political Islam. Islamic financial law, which is essential to any deep understanding of Islamic society, is familiar only to a few insiders. And only slowly are the Muslims themselves correcting the many misunderstandings that exist about their life-practice.

This crisis across Europe offers a historic opportunity for Muslims living there. There have been numerous reports about the Muslims' position, vis-à-vis economic issues, and what the Shari'a says about it, and this has created a certain degree of interest. For the first time, Islam has been able to show itself in this area as part of a solution rather than part of a problem. Examined more closely, the basic economic principles of Islam are in fact highly reasonable.

The worship of capitalism which established itself across the continent after the fall of communism is now giving way to an atmosphere of serious doubt and a search for alternatives. The philosopher Walter Benjamin criticised the quasi-religious aspect of capitalism, noting that capitalism serves to "assuage the same anxieties, agonies and unease which so-called religions once gave answer to." In other words, the Enlightenment had finally reached the Western economic model.

It was perhaps the Italian intellectual, Loretta Napoleoni, who first recognised the new situation, and seeing something positive in Islam. In the 1990s, following the reunification of Germany, she wrote a book called "Rogue Economics" which explained the devastating effects of capitalism now that it had broken out of all limits. In this book the journalist recognises Islam as an inspiring form of moderated economic activity.

Although Napoleoni has actually been known as a critic of Islam, some years later in the newspaper,

"Osservatore Romana," she stated respectfully about Islamic economic law: "We believe that Islamic finance can contribute to the establishment of new rules for Western finance... Shari'a-compliant investment forms prevent the artificial generation of money." It was an important point she had raised.

## 1. Opportunities

The presence of more than 54 million Muslims in Europe has of course meant that many non-Muslim Europeans have come to know about some aspects of Islamic practice. Most Europeans know that Muslims do not eat pork or drink alcohol, and that they consider this to be part of a divinely ordained way of life. People also know that certain things may be allowed and other things forbidden in a religion, but that such rules might play a decisive role in everyday economic transactions remains hidden from people of other religions or no religion at all. This is despite the fact that Christianity and Judaism for much of their history forbade the taking of interest just as Islam does.

The foremost principle which we Muslims must now convey is that the Shari'a, far from being some kind or irrational system of coercion, intends above all to prevent what is harmful and encourage what is beneficial to human beings. Since the Creator placed everything on this earth at the disposal of people, one of the basic principles of Islam is that all things are permitted except if they are explicitly forbidden by the Shari'a. This means that Islam is a life-practice which makes things easier, establishing a middle-way rather than extremes. This is also why the Quran warns specifically against forbidding things which are allowed.

In this context it is often forgotten that as well as a food having to be "halal", it should also be "tayyib", which means "good." So what is at issue is not only how something is slaughtered, but also that food – and of course animals – are handled well and sensibly. Furthermore, as well as Muslims expecting their foods to be permitted, they also want them to have been fairly traded and properly paid for. The Quranic injunction to trade "by mutual agreement" today translates quite simply as "fair trade."

Because we believe that the rules of Islam make sense today as they did in the past, we Muslims must participate confidently in the public discussion on an economically viable system of supply. There are great opportunities here for the Muslims of Europe to position themselves advantageously. Globally, more than 2.1 billion Muslims are potentially networked in a halal market, and they represent enormous spending power and economic potential.

World Muslim consumers, according to surveys, cannot be properly categorised as either liberal or conservative. Instead they are motivated and ambitious, globally thinking, educated and optimistic, and open to technical innovations. But they are also upholders of family traditions, pro-community, preservers of their cultures – and, not least, they enjoy practicing Islam. This applies in Asia and America just as it does in Europe. It may be those Muslims in Europe, who have studied European philosophy and its critique of technology, are less apt to believe wholeheartedly in that technology than those who have not.

Islam's economic position and the growing market for halal products and services did not really become a topic of any importance in Europe until relatively recently. This is somewhat surprising given that most of the major

legal books devote hundreds of pages to contracts, market laws and fundamental economic rulings. The Quran mentions not only the prayer but also the taking of zakat, which is an obligatory, if moderate, wealth tax. There is no doubt that this is a most intriguing aspect of Islam.

The theme of "Islam and economics" deserves much more attention for several reasons. The millions of Muslims who live in Europe, in other words the masses of native and immigrant Muslim consumers, represent a growing economic force. Fourteen million Muslims live in the European Union, 4.3 and 5.4 million of which live in the economically strongest nations of Germany and France respectively. All of these people invest, buy and save, and – this being the next aspect – they do so observing particular economic rulings.

Islamic economic law, of which the regulations of the halal market are but a part, represents a web of rules, standards and prohibitions which in its totality deserves recognition as an alternative economy. It involves much more than just stipulations about the production of food. In Islam, business life must be built around a free market, fair trade and free trade routes; without this framework, many of Islam's rules do not make any sense.

The combination of economic power and knowledge which the Muslims have therefore represents an enormous potential, since with some intelligence they can demonstrate new ways of doing things and propose important alternatives, enabling Muslims to be perceived in Europe as the pioneers of a complete alternative economy. Only as business people and producers, only as fair traders and upright suppliers will the Muslims present in Europe be received positively by the non-Muslim majority societies. This will bring with it an urgently needed makeover of the Muslim image.

Global demand for halal food is rising, with some estimating that demand will increase by a rate of 20% each year from now until 2025. The importance of the European market is also growing steadily. The European market for halal food products currently has a volume of approximately USD66 billion, and the markets of Germany and France have a particularly large untapped potential. The Canadian Global Pathfinder Report on Halal Food Trends reported in 2009-2010 on more than 40 newly launched halal products in Germany and France alone.

The question is how to convert these encouraging facts into positive outcomes for Muslims, and who in the end will actually profit from the economic potential of this market. There are certain problems which need to be recognized and discussed openly.

## 2. Problems

There are of course many difficulties surrounding what is in itself the positive scenario of the Muslims' purchasing power. Muslims are far from united when it comes to the halal business. They argue about how legal rulings ought to be applied, and they remain divided into national camps, and torn between differing religious interests. As a result, Muslim representatives have neither a common strategy nor an agreed-upon marketing concept.

Nor are people very aware that the halal market, aside from food, also encompasses many other principles and areas of business. There are of course efforts directed towards opening a market in financial products and insurance, but often these involve simply copying other institutions and giving them a religious tone by appending the "Islamic" before the product or service. Few people have actually considered setting up a genuine Islamic market, or reviving some of tried-and-tested financial instruments. Not only is there a lack of Islamic infrastructure, there is also a need for an up- to-date, convincing portrayal of the entirety of Islamic economic concepts, starting from the type and role of money, market regulations, and the products which are acceptable for purchase.

It is important that Muslims do not simply adopt seemingly successful sales strategies without understanding the negative effects these mechanisms can have. Supermarkets are a case in point. One must bear in mind that the Prophet himself established in Medina a mosque and a market, both of which were public institutions and both of which offered equal access to everyone. For many centuries it was unthinkable that just a few suppliers would dominate a market. The traditional Islamic market was open to thousands of suppliers. In Germany, the food market is dominated by just a few discounters, and the idea of free trade has long fallen by the wayside. The owner of the largest food chain in Germany is regularly at the top of the list of the country's richest people. It may well be that even these discounters one day introduce "halal departments," but would that really satisfy the principles of fair trade in Islam?

It is certainly essential that people become more aware of the diversity and complexity of Islamic trade activities. Contributing towards such a growth in awareness are not only the Islamic media, but also large-scale exhibitions such as the Euro halal market in Brussels and the Paris Halal Expo in Paris. These events quickly demonstrate that Muslims are active not only locally but also within a broader context. They show that the Muslims are internationally networked, and they are also a door for European manufacturers who wish to supply the global Muslim market. Only if the significance of halal regulations within an overall economy is made clear can we avoid creating the impression that Muslims have nothing more than a narrow expertise in the food area.

The halal market in Europe still bears the stigma of exotic slaughtering practices for some Europeans. A fierce conflict of beliefs has also erupted between animal welfare activists on the one hand and Muslims and Jews on the other. Conservative groupings in Europe, some of which are Islamophobic, have attempted to vilify Islam and Judaism as being backwards in regard to animal welfare, and a love of animals is often only a pretext to fight. These are groupings that have used the growing fear of Islam among Europeans skillfully to their own ends. One of the challenges now facing Muslims is to conduct intelligently a dialogue clarifying the relation between Islam and animal welfare, and to make plain the worries many Muslims have about animals being kept and slaughtered in an inappropriate way.

At the same time Muslims have to take a position in the general discussion about industrial food production. The issues that arise are very clear for all to see. For example, can mass animal rearing really be compatible with Divine legislation?

Another major problem facing the young halal market is the ferocious power struggle taking place around the subject of certification. As in other regions, Europe has seen an increase in the number of cases in which certified meat has in fact not been slaughtered correctly at all. Cases of certification abuse may be isolated but they still need to be taken seriously. And many "Islamic" certifying bodies, plenty of which are active only on the Internet, are of dubious legitimacy. They have been cases of retailers that have utilised an invented halal logo, that has not been approved by a authoritative halal body, to sell meat as it was easier to distribute in certain countries.

In some Muslim countries the legitimization of certifiers is government regulated on a national level, whereas in Europe, certification tends to be in the hands of a bewildering number of private entities. That is why Muslims in Europe are also discussing whether centralized certification would improve things. There is however good cause for skepticism here, since centralization is liable to remain a utopia for many reasons. The complicated division and subdivision of Muslims in Europe along ethical and religious lines makes it unlikely that any such authority will emerge in the foreseeable future.

Serious certifiers may well share much common ground, but there are of course differences between the legal schools, as is evidenced by the ongoing debate about anesthesia. Looking to Muslims countries for certification also brings difficulties: why should consumers in Europe defer to authorities abroad?

There is another serious problem with the torrent of certification, which we shall touch upon only briefly. People often point out that centralized certification only really strengthens the big multinationals and weakens small suppliers, even if they are operating correctly as Muslims, because it encourages expensive overregulation and promotes a distrust of non-certified products. It is hard to dismiss this argument entirely.

And today it is indeed Western food corporations who dominate the global food market. One good example is the company Nestlé. This Swiss firm has been offering halal products as far back as 1980. Of the Group's 443 factories, no less than 85 are halal certified. The Group's strategists process the international market from offices in Malaysia. Their products for the Islamic world are worth more than 5 billion Swiss francs and constitute 5% of annual turnover. Experts like Dr Paul Temporal may bemoan the lack of Western companies' market expertise when it comes to halal products, but he surely cannot be referring to these Swiss operators. This all means of course a growing influence on the certification institutions by a small number of big players. In the long term it cannot be in Muslims' interest that only a few monopolists dominate the food market.

## 3. Challenges

One of the things Muslims in Europe have so far failed to do is to properly realize their own potential. There is to date no central body able to provide sound information about the economic strength of the Muslims. It is almost impossible to obtain accurate figures, statistics and market analyses.

Nor have the opportunities which the internet holds for the European halal market been exhausted by any stretch of the imagination. However, there are glimmers of change. The Salamworld1 initiative hopes to build up a social network similar to Facebook. If the project is successful then this will have positive consequences for the halal market, given its 50 million hoped-for users. It is time for there to be a virtual marketplace on the Internet, and for Islamic contract models to be offered, and even an alternative payment system. But the Internet will make an exclusively European strategy almost impossible.

Given the relentless march of globalization, it is of course important for Muslims to firm up their legal convictions in the face of ever mightier market forces.

So far Muslims have been relatively uncritical of food corporations, supermarkets and banks in comparison with other European citizens. The Islamic world has remained strangely quiet about the configuration of money, monopolies and banks. European society has been discussing such relationships openly for a long time. A critical review is long overdue now that we have reached the 21st century, especially a review of what people refer to as Islamic financial instruments.

It is well known that in the second Sura of Qur'an, trade is allowed and riba is forbidden, which means from a Muslim's point of view that monopolistic distribution by a small number of large chains is as unacceptable as the circumvention of a prohibition on interest by crafty banks. Attempts to distort the law are especially rife in the world of finance. The big Islamic banks and insurance companies view Europe as a large market, quite naturally. The Islamic Bank of Britain already had 8 branches and 42,000 clients by the year 2007, and held investments amounting to more than 135 million pounds.

The first ever purely Islamic bank from Turkey aims to set up shop in Germany in 2013. Muslims in Germany alone are estimated to possess assets worth more than

25 billion euros, but this money is threatened by rising inflation rates. Just because a bank titles itself "Islamic" it does not automatically mean that it operates in harmony with Islamic financial laws.

In Germany, Islamic banks are trying to operate in the property market by means of contracts that circumvent the prohibition on interest by combining two consecutive sales agreements in one, but this arrangement, ironically, has so stumbled on German tax laws. Imam Malik, among others, expressly forbade this kind of obviously double-sale transaction.

Germany's banking supervisory body BaFin has praised Islamic banks for coming out of the financial crisis relatively unharmed, and because they stay more or less away from risky transactions, but despite this they

remain in essence normal banks like any other. They have long been intermeshed with the non-Islamic banking system through speculation and complex business relationships. In Germany, the Central Muslim Council has certified what it says is a halal product issued by WestLB, a bank which only recently had to be rescued from collapse using millions of euros of taxpayers' money.

Muslim jurists will not be able to escape the lessons of the banking crisis and the growing doubt people have in the relationship between banks and the creation of money. There is now a broad and fundamental discussion going on in Europe between Muslims, Christians and Jews: "Is it legitimate for banks to create money practically out of nothing?"

A growing number of Europeans are doubting this legitimacy regardless of their confession, and even German Bundestag members such as FDP politician Franz Schäffler are demanding the legalization of private currencies. "Only then," argues this politician, "will nation- states be prevented from printing more and more false money."

Muslims are well positioned to consider the legal possibilities of reintroducing their coinage into circulation, meaning Dinars and Dirhams, which are 100% gold and silver backed and which have been part of the Islamic economy for centuries. Considering the crisis among European insurers, gold-back savings accounts – known as wadiya – would be a secure option for Muslims and non-Muslims alike. But the Muslims have not quite grasped these opportunities in the financial market as yet. Perhaps the greatest challenge facing the future halal market will be to learn from the current crisis and to place more trust once again in the soundness of our own financial instruments. After the experience of communism and financial capitalism, the task is to find a third way, which is the middle way. Owning property and intending to make profits are both honorable intentions in Islam, but the law must prevent monopolies and guarantee fair competition.

## References

1. Abojeib, M., & Habib, F. (2019). Blockchain for Islamic Social Responsibility Institutions FinTech as a Disruptive Technology for Financial Institutions (pp. 221-240): IGI Global.
2. Ager, S. N. S., et al. AN ANALYSIS OF THE DEFINITION OF HALAL:SHARI'AH VS STATUTES. World Academic and Research Congress 2015 (World-AR 2015) Ar-Rahim Hall, YARSI University, Jakarta, Indonesia, 9th – 10th December 2015.
3. Awang, R., et al. (2014). "Halal epistemology from a global perspective." Social Sciences (Pakistan) 9(6).
4. Berryhill, J., T. Bourgery and A. Hanson. (2018). Blockchains Unchained: Blockchain Technology and its Use in the Public Sector by I F N F i n Te c h.
5. Dali, N., et al. (2007). HALAL PRODUCTS FROM THE CONSUMERS PERCEPTION. AN ONLINE SURVEY. Proceeding of the Islamic Entrepreneurship Conference, KolejUniversiti Islam Malaysia.

6. Dar, H., et al. (2013). Global Islamic Finance Report: GIFR 2013, Edbiz Consulting.
7. Dewar, J., & Hussain, M. M. (2011). ISLAMIC PROJECT FINANCE. In J. Dewar (Ed.), International Project Finance: Law and Practice: OUP Oxford.
8. Di Mauro, F., Caristi, P., Couderc, S., Di Maria, A., Ho, L., Grewal, B. K., . . . Zaher, S. (2013). Islamic finance in Europe. Retrieved from
9. Drescher, D. (2017). Blockchain Basics: A Non-technical Introduction in 25 Steps, 1st edn. Apress, Frankfurt am Main (2017).
10. Elasrag, H. (9. April 2011). Principals of the Islamic finance: A focus on project finance. MPRA Paper No. 30197.
11. Fleishman Hillard Majlis (2011). "The Market Opportunity of the Muslim World."
12. Ghuddah, A. S. A. (1998). Ijarah (lease). Dallah Al-Baraka Group Al-Baraka Banking Group (ABG) Department of Research & Development.
13. Gupta , L., & Alam, N. (2019). Blockchain-Driven Remittance:Opportunities for Islamic Finance. I-FIKR DIGEST SPECIAL I(SSUE 1).
14. Hasni bin Wan Sulaiman, W. M. (2017). Islamic

Finance and the Blockchain Revolution. Paper presented at the Cryptocurrency, Blockchain & Distributed Ledger Technology: Synergizing Technology & Shariah, Kulliyyah of ICT, IIUM.

15. Hj Hassan, F. (2013). Halal food marketing: dare to win! Malaysia, UiTM Press.
16. International Finance Corporation. (2019). Blockchain : Opportunities for Private Enterprises in Emerging Markets, Second Edition. International Finance Corporation. Retrieved from Washington, DC.: https://openknowledge.worldbank.org/handle/10986/31251
17. Iqbal, Z. (1997). Islamic financial systems. Finance and Development, 34, 42-45.
18. Kamali, M. H. (2010). "The halal industry from a shari'ah perspective." Islam and Civilisational Renewal 1(4.
19. Kamali, M. H. (2012). "Tourism and the Halal Industry: A Global Shariah Perspective." Islam and Civilizational Renewal (ICR) 3(3).
20. Malboobi, M. T. and M. A. Malboobi (2012). Halal concept and products derived from modern biotechnology. International workshop for Islamic

scholars on agribiotechnology: Shariah compliance.

21. Mohamed, H., & Ali, H. (2018). Blockchain, Fintech, and Islamic Finance: Building the Future in the New Islamic Digital Economy: Walter de Gruyter GmbH & Co KG.
22. Mougayar, W. (2016). The business blockchain: promise, practice, and application of the next Internet technology: John Wiley & Sons.
23. Muhammada, M. Z., & Chonga, R. (2007). The Contract of Bay'Al-Salam and Istisna' in Islamic Commercial Law: A comparative analysis. Labuan e-Journal of Muamalat and Society, 1, 21-28.
24. Muhammed , H. (KLCC 30 March – 4 April 2015). Halal: Defining Terms, Educating Communities. MIHAS: The Halal Global Market Place – World Halal Summit.
25. Rana, O., & Akinlaso, M. I. (Q3 2018). How Blockchain can impact the Muslim world: Food S&P Shariah Indices Methodology, (March 2014).
26. Sadouskaya, K. (2017). Adoption of Blockchain Technology in Supply Chain and Logistics.
27. Salaam Gateway (JANUARY 2016). "Muslim-Friendly Beach Resorts: Opportunities and

Trends." Monthly Report Series Prepared.

28. Sultan, K., Ruhi, U., & Lakhani, R. (2018). Conceptualizing Blockchains: Characteristics & Applications. Paper presented at the 11th IADIS International Conference Information Systems
29. Sylvester, G. ( 2019). E-agriculture in action: Blockchain for agriculture
30. Tan, B., Yan, J., Chen, S., & Liu, X. (2018). The Impact of Blockchain on Food Supply Chain: The Case of Walmart. Paper presented at the International Conference on Smart Blockchain.
31. Thomson Reuters and Dinar Standard (2016). "State of the Global Islamic Economy 2015/16 Report." Thomson Reuters and Dinar Standard, New York City.
32. Tieman, M., & Darun, M. R. (2017). Leveraging blockchain technology for halal supply chains. Islam and Civilizational Renewal (ICR), 8(4), 547-550.
33. Zakaria, Z. (2008). "Tapping into the world halal market: some discussions on Malaysian laws and standards." Shariah Journal 16(3.

www.ingramcontent.com/pod-product-compliance
Ingram Content Group UK Ltd.
Pitfield, Milton Keynes, MK11 3LW, UK
UKHW020158290926
15471UKWH00005B/945

9 788664 368612